THE BIG BOOK OF HOW WHEN & WHY?

Original Italian text and editorial content: Laura Tassi
Production editor: Stefano Sibella
Graphics and covers: Viviana Cerrato
Pagination: Marco and Matteo Volpati (Fox Studio)
Editor; technical content: Gianluigi Ronchetti
Picture research: Laura Tassi, Frederica Magrin

Illustrations supplied by picture agencies:
Photographs and drawings, DeAgostini Picture Library:
Photograph, p96 - Marco Volpati
Photographs, pp. 44, 55, 64, 70, 74, 137, 171, 175, 176 - Frederica Magrin

Il Grande Libro delle Domande & Risposte

ISBN 978-0-7097-2225-0

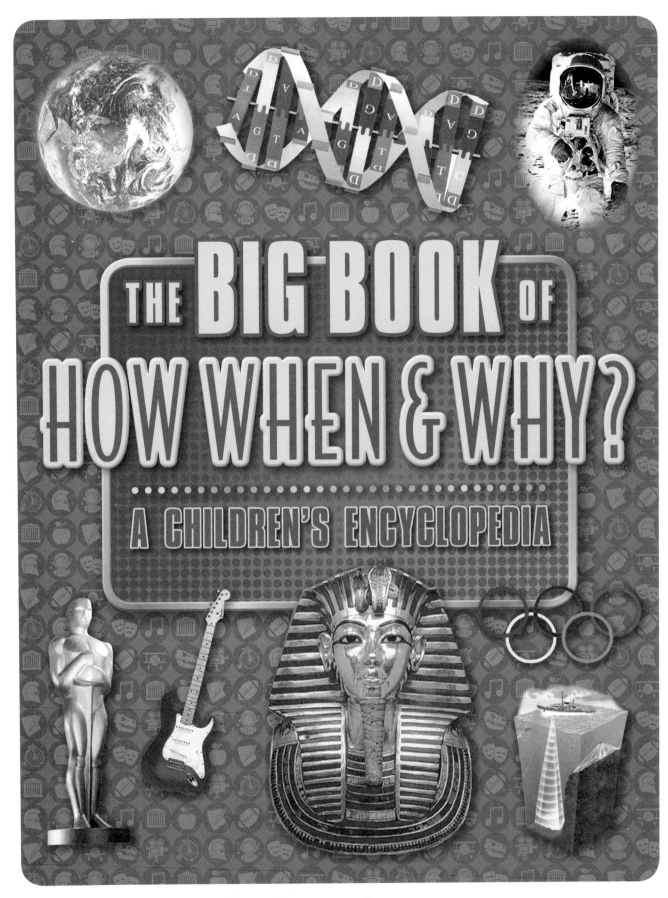

THE BIG BOOK OF HOW WHEN & WHY?

A CHILDREN'S ENCYCLOPEDIA

Brown Watson

ENGLAND

CONTENTS

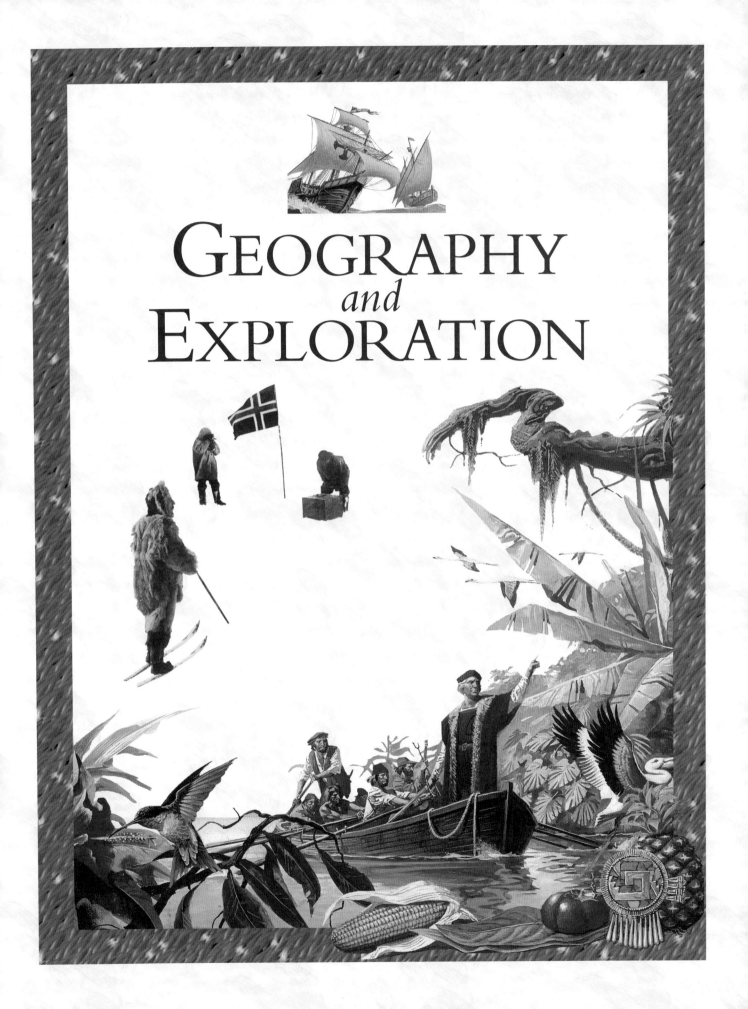

GEOGRAPHY
and
EXPLORATION

When were the first maps drawn?
Who drew them?

The **earliest map** found by archeologists was drawn about **15,000 years ago**. This ancient map, discovered in **Mezin** in the Ukraine depicted an encampment and a river which flowed nearby. Another ancient and important piece of evidence is the **Stone of Jebel Amud**, discovered in southern Jordan and drawn between *10,000* and *6,000* years ago. This also maps out an inhabited settlement. Even before they learned to read and write, people were aware of the necessity to draw and to describe their own territories. Early maps were first carved on stone, and then on clay tablets by the Ancient Babylonians. The earliest tablet discovered so far dates from 2,400 – 2,200 years ago and was discovered at **Gar-Sur**, about 400 km to the north of **Babylon**. This maps out the course of a river, thought to be the Euphrates, and some inhabited areas.

The map of the world, according to the Egyptian astronomer and mathematician Ptolemy

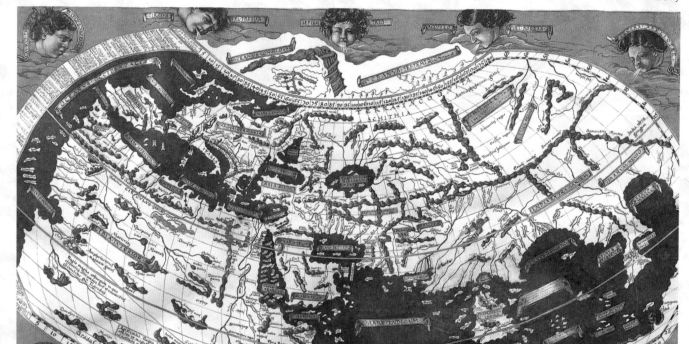

The second clay tablet discovered (**the tablet of Nippur**, *top right*) is a map of Nippur, an ancient city of Mesopotamia. The third is the Babylon 'mappamondo' (map of the world) found at Uruk and depicting the Earth as a circle surrounded by water and with Babylon at the centre.

Did You Know...

The first person to draw maps of the Earth which took its curved surface into account was the Flemish geographer **Gerhard Kremer** (Latin name Gerardus Mercator). In 1569, he re-drew the map of the world as if our planet was a cylinder unrolled on to a flat surface. This was called 'Mercator's projection' and it became the basis for all maps. It was also a great aid to navigation, because it enabled sailors and explorers to identify the simplest route from one place to another and to keep on track. Before the nautical maps of Kremer, navigators used their '**pilot books**', a book of small maps on which were drawn the ports and the coast, with information on the weather, tides, currents and levels of water and local trading.

Map of the world with Babylon at the centre

The map of Europe, according to Ptolemy

What was the 'Silk Road'?

The '**Silk Road**' (or the 'Silk Route') was a long and ancient route which connected **eastern Asia** (*Peking*) to **Europe** (*Istanbul*).
The first to follow the Silk Road and to draw maps of it were the Chinese merchants who traded with Europe, bringing valuable goods such as silk and spices, in exchange for silver, gold and horses. The merchants who travelled along the Silk Road needed plenty of courage. Many places were almost impassable and dangerous and temperatures varied from one extreme to another. Near the **Gobi Desert** the heat was suffocating and the only possibility of surviving was to stop near the oases which were scattered along through the desert and which provided the travellers with food and water. In the mountainous areas of the Himalayas, the merchants had to cope with freezing cold temperatures, as well as climbing the hazardous passes which were often blocked by snow.

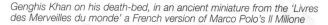

A small part of the Silk Road

Genghis Khan on his death-bed, in an ancient miniature from the 'Livres des Merveilles du monde' a French version of Marco Polo's Il Milione

Ancient miniature showing Marco Polo at the palace of Kublai Khan

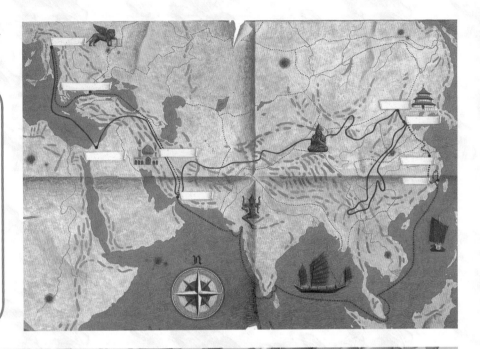

Stops along Marco Polo's adventurous journey

HOW LONG WAS IT?

About **7000 km**, whilst the journey from Peking to the great city of Samarcanda, an important stop along the way, lasted about six months. The route began to be made around 500 BC and came to be used as the only link between Europe and the East until 1650. After that, the shortest and safest way was by sea.

A FAMOUS TRAVELLER...

At only 17 years of age, **Marco Polo** together with his father Niccolò and his uncle Matteo, went in 1271 to China by way of the Silk Route. The famous stories of his journey are told in the book *Il Milione* (subtitle, *The Travels of Marco Polo*). The title of this book came from *Emilione*, the name which the Polo family used to distinguish them from other Venetian houses. The book was written and published in French with various titles – *Divisament du monde* or *Livres des merveilles du monde*, as well as, in Latin, *De mirabilibus mundi*. The original text of the book was lost and so each version read today is a mixture of different traditions.

The city of Venice, where Marco Polo sailed from, in an ancient miniature

Who discovered America?

On 3 August 1492, the Italian explorer **Christopher Columbus**, financed by the Spanish king and queen, Ferdinand II of Aragon and Isabela of Castile, sailed from the port of **Palos** in Spain, captaining a fleet of three caravelles – the **Niña**, the **Pinta** and the **Santa Maria**. Columbus, believing the age-old theories about the Earth being round, embarked on the voyage to try and find a new sea route to India. He was convinced that he would reach the legendary Orient by travelling east. On **11 October 1492**, after two months of exhausting navigation, he reached dry land – not that of the mythical Asia, but a new continent – Hispanic America, or the Caribbean as we know it today. In this first expedition, Columbus discovered and explored the **Guanahani Islands** (afterwards re-named San Salvador in the Bahamas), Cuba and Haiti.

HOW MUCH DID COLOMBUS KNOW?

Christopher Columbus based his scientific theories on the wrong presumptions. He believed the world was round, but with a circumference much smaller than it actually is. So, he thought that, by sailing west, it would be possible to get from Spain to Japan with a voyage of around 5000 km, instead of the 20000 km which it proved to be. He had also under-estimated the vastness of the Atlantic Ocean or the **Western Sea**, as it was called at that time.

Christopher Columbus exploring the luxuriant coast of the island of Cuba

WHAT HAPPENED TO THE CARAVELLES?

The beautiful caravelle the **Santa Maria** (150 tonnes in weight) was shipwrecked after touching the coast of Haiti, forcing part of the crew to remain on the island, where they built a fortress which they called **Navidad**. Columbus and the other sailors had to return to Spain on the 15 March 1493 on board the one remaining caravelle, the **Niña** (the smallest ship, weighing 100 tonnes). At Cuba, the **Pinta** (140 tonnes in weight) captained by Alonso Pinzón, became separated from the other caravelles and proceeded alone in search of new lands and riches.

THE INHERITANCE OF THE NEW WORLD

In the New World (later called the West Indies), Columbus and his men discovered new customs, clothes and foods. **Sweet potatoes** and **pineapple**, everyday foods to the native people, were quite unknown in Europe, as well as sweet peppers, beans, tomatoes and corn. Columbus also saw that the 'New World Indians', as he called them, slept on **hammocks** which they hung from the trees. He installed hammocks in his ships, which the sailors found much more comfortable than sleeping on hard ground.

WHEN WAS THE FIRST MAP OF AMERICA DRAWN?

The first geographical map of America was made in 1507, 15 years after the voyage of Christopher Columbus. It was drawn by **Martin Waldseemüller** and it is now owned by the Library of Congress, Washington, DC.

WHICH COUNTRY'S NAVIGATORS REACHED NORTH AMERICA BEFORE COLUMBUS?

Many historians say that when the ancient Norse legends are read and examined carefully, it can be seen that the Viking people knew the American continent long before the discovery by Columbus. The **Viking Leif Eriksson** is known to have landed in America around 1000 AD, losing track of his route whilst going to Greenland.

Circular quadrants, ancient instruments used by sailors to find their way

A typical Viking ship with a square sail

The Viking ship Knar setting sail for Greenland

Who discovered the ruins of Troy?

In 1871 **Heinrich Schliemann** (1822-1890) astounded the world by discovering the ruins of Troy. From a young student, he had cherished the dream of finding this legendary city. At the age of ten, he had written an essay in Latin on the Trojan Wars and of the heroes who had taken part. His family thought this to be a typical teenage craze, but Heinrich never gave up. Fifty years later he succeeded in making that dream come true. He worked with the collaboration of committed experts such as Rudolf Virchow and Wilhelm Dörpfeld, with whom he shared joys and sorrows.

Heinrich Schliemann

Thanks also to the work of another student, **C. W. Blegen** who proceeded with the excavations (1932-1938) **new layers** beneath the **old city** were discovered, providing links to periods of history which had been previously unknown. According to Blegen, the numerous layers matched up with the mythical city of Troy, described by the poet **Homer** in his epic works the *Iliad* and the *Odyssey*. Because of his wonderful discovery, Heinrich Schliemann is seen as the father of modern archaeology. Before him, archaeologists had excavated the site mainly to discover objects of art, vases and pictures. Never before had anyone been driven to search for the city and civilization which had disappeared.

WHO FOUNDED TROY?

Legend says that the city was founded by **Dardanus** son of god **Zeus** and **Electra**, one of the Pleiades, the 'seven sisters'. From Dardanus descended the dynasty of the Trojans or 'Dardanians'. After its foundation, they ruled Troy – Erichthonius, Troilus, Ilos, Laomedon and Priam. From the reign of **Troilus** the city was called Troy and from the reign of Ilos it became Ilion, the other name by which it was known in ancient times.

The treasure of King Priam

The wall of the city of Troy

When were the Victoria Falls discovered?

In November **1855**, David Livingstone discovered an enormous fall of water which he called the **Victoria Falls** in honour of the Queen of Great Britain.

The Zambesi River

The Victoria Falls

Queen Victoria

WHERE DID THE VICTORIA FALLS START FROM?

It is the Zambesi River which 'feeds' the Victoria Falls. David Livingstone was the first to discover the river, during one of his many explorations. Tracking the upper reaches of the Zambesi, he succeeded in finding the exact point at which the river, by tumbling down through a narrow gorge, gushes out into the famous waterfall. Its main jump, called 'booming smoke' by the Makololo natives, is 122 metres high. Livingstone drew a map of the course of the Zambesi and the Victoria Falls which was so precise that even today it is still being used without the risk of anyone losing the way!

WHO WAS DAVID LIVINGSTONE?

Scottish-born David Livingstone (1813-1873) was a missionary and a British explorer. In 1840, he graduated in medicine and became a member of the London Missionary Society. He was sent to Kuruman in Africa, with the purpose of founding missions and spreading the Christian faith. But because of his great love for the 'Black Continent', he abandoned strictly religious tasks in order to become a great explorer. He was the **first European to cross Africa** from one coast to the other in a **journey** which stretched him to impossible limits and which lasted **three years** (1853-1856). Leaving Kuruman, a small town south of the Kalahari Desert, he reached the Zambesi River and decided to follow its course to the west. On 31 May 1854 he arrived at San Paolo in Luanda, Angola, on the Atlantic coast, accompanied only by his faithful bearers from the Makolo people. Then he went on to follow the course of the river, this time towards the east and in May 1856 reached the Indian Ocean, at Quelimane. Most of the journey he undertook on foot, discovering the wonderful Victoria Falls on the way.

David Livingstone

Who defined the Greenwich meridian as zero longitude?

In **1881**, during the third International Geographical Congress, some famous geographers put forward the proposal of adopting the Greenwich meridian line as zero (0°) longitude, with the purpose of setting this longitude and its time as a point of reference for all countries. The idea was not accepted at once by all countries and it was only in **1884**, at the **International Geographical Congress in Washington** that the issue was raised again. This time, it was accepted by everyone. 'Greenwich time' came into force in **1912** at the **First International Conference on Time**.

WHAT IS GREENWICH?

Greenwich is a **suburb of London** to the south of the River Thames. In 1675, the famous Royal Observatory was founded here. The Observatory is no longer used for astronomical purpose, but it is still important because this is where the **longitude zero (0°) passes through**.

SEVEN HOURS DIFFERENCE...

Some countries, such as the United States, Russia and Canada are so vast that there are great differences between time zones within the same country. For instance – in Russia, if in Moscow it was 20:00 pm, in Vladivostok, also in Russia, at that same instant it would be 3:00 am the next day. Some nations between two time zones adopt time zones which are peculiar to them, and which differ by adding an extra half hour or a quarter hour to Greenwich time. For example, to determine the time in Nepal, we need to add to Greenwich time five hours and 45 minutes.

The Royal Observatory, Greenwich

HOW MANY TIME ZONES ARE THERE IN THE WORLD?

There are **24** time zones in the world. This signifies that the Earth is divided into 24 'slices', and each time zone moves on one hour from the previous time zone and each 'slice' is 15° wide. Time zone **one** is that of Greenwich and, universal time (**UT**) which serves as a reference for the whole world, is calculated from this. To the west of Greenwich (towards America) the time decreases; to the east (towards Asia and Australia) the time increases. So, if at Greenwich it is only 11 o'clock in the morning, at New York, it will be 6 o'clock in the morning, whilst at Sydney it will be 21:00 hrs (9 o'clock) in the evening.

WHERE IS DEATH VALLEY?

It is in California. It is a place without any water and where the temperature is so high (in 1913, **57°** was registered) that all forms of life struggle to survive. This is why it is called **Death Valley**.

Death Valley

WHERE IS THERE A MOUNTAIN HIGHER THAN EVEREST?

Mount Everest is 8849.86 metres high. But there is a higher mountain, partly beneath the waters of the Pacific Ocean. It is called **Mauna Kea** and it is an **ancient volcano** of Hawaii, now extinct. If we consider also the part submerged by the waters of the Pacific, Mauna Key has an altitude of **9754 metres**.

An active volcano on the island of Hawaii

WHERE IS THE LONGEST ROAD IN THE WORLD?
This is in America and it is called the **Pan-American Highway**. *It is a super-highway of 22,300 kilometres which begins at Anchorage in Alaska and finishes near Terra del Fuoco in southern America.*

HOW MANY YEARS OLD IS THE MOST ANCIENT CITY IN THE WORLD?
The remains of the oldest city has no name. It was found at a depth of 40 metres in the Gulf of Cambay, in north-west India and dates back to 75,000 BC.

WHERE IS THE MOST VAST OCEAN?

The most vast ocean is the **Pacific**. It has a surface area of 179,650,000 km² (square kilometres), washing the coasts of northern, central and south America, Australia and eastern Asia.

The Pacific Ocean

WHERE IS THE LONGEST RIVER?

The **Nile** is the longest river in the world. It is 6,671 kilometres long and flows through four countries of eastern Africa (Uganda, Sudan, Ethiopia and Egypt). The name of the Nile changes slightly as it continues its course, so that it is sometimes called the **Albert Nile**, the **Nile of the Mountains**, the **White Nile** and the **Blue Nile**.

The Nile

When was the Pacific Ocean discovered?

Vasco Nuñez de Balboa

The Spanish explorer Vasco **Nuñez de Balboa** discovered the Pacific Ocean. After setting out from America following the conqueror Rodrigo de Bastidas, he decided to sail towards the **Isthmus of Darién** (called the Isthmus of Panama today) in Central America. From here, with a following of 600 natives and 200 Spanish soldiers, he undertook a dangerous journey on foot through tropical forest. This journey lasted a month, and on 29 September 1513, he reached a previously undiscovered ocean which he called **Mar del Sur** (the southern sea).

The first to reach the Pacific by sea was the Portuguese Navigator **Ferdinand Magellan**. In the service of the Spanish King Carlo V, Magellan succeeded in reaching India by sailing towards the west, along a route to the south of the American continent. Leaving **Sanlùcar de Barrameda** in Spain on **20 September 1519**, he led his five ships and 277 men towards South America. During the voyage, the ship Santiago was wrecked, leaving few survivors.

The crew of another ship, the Sant' Antonio mutinied and returned to Spain. The three remaining ships sailed towards the extreme point of South America, today called the **Straits of Magellan**, crossing through and finding themselves in very calm waters, which they called the Sea of Peace or the Pacific (meaning 'peaceful') Ocean. Magellan continued his voyage and in 1521 reached the **Marianne Islands** and the Philippines. Here, Magellan was killed on 27 April during a confrontation with the natives. The crew of the one remaining ship, the **Victoria**, returned to **Sanlùcar de Barrameda** in **1522**, three years after they had left.

FERDIN · MAGELLANVS · SVPERATIS ANTARTICᵛ TIIS · FRETI · ANGVS CLARISS ·

Ferdinand Magellan

DID THE VICTORIA RETURN ON THE 5TH OR THE 6TH OF SEPTEMBER 1522?

The **navigator's calendar** recorded Saturday **5 September 1522** as the day of the return of the Victoria, whilst at Sanlùcar de Barrameda, the calendar showed Sunday **6 September**. **How could this have happened?** The explanation is actually very simple! The expedition chose a route with an east-to-west direction, so that they could sail in the same direction as the sun. But, as the Earth turned on its axis, the rising sun would be seen one time less by them than at Sanlùcar.

THE FEAR OF CARLO V
King Carlo V of Spain *refused to eat* **pineapple** *when these were offered to him the first time, for fear that they were poisonous fruit*

Spanish galleons captained by Magellan reach the wild coast of Patagonia

When was Australia explored?

Between 1860 and 1861 the expedition led by the brave **Robert O'Hara Burke**, **William Wills**, **Charles Gray** and **John King** explored Australia from the south to the north. The departure was fixed at **Port Phillip**, now Melbourne, at the south of Australia. These four European explorers plus another three men in the team, left on the backs of camels. They preferred these to horses when travelling in hot climates, because camels can store and conserve precious water.

After three months of travelling they reached **Cooper Creek**, at the mouth of the River Cooper. This place was chosen as a base to deposit the provisions and three members of the expedition decided to stop there and to wait for the return of the others. In February 1861, Burke, Wills, Grey and King reached the **Gulf of Carpentaria**, to the north of the continent, completely exhausted. But tragedy struck during the return journey. Grey, Burke and Willis died of hunger and thirst, whilst King was only saved because he was found by aborigines who helped him to recover.

Aborigine dance

WHO ARE THE TRUE INHABITANTS OF AUSTRALIA?

The Aborigines are the true Australian natives. It is thought that they emigrated from south-east Asia 30,000 years ago to settle in Australia. They are divided into various groups, the most important of which are the **Kulin**, the **Cepara**, the **Kurnai** and the **Aranda**. With the arrival of white settlers from about 1800, the Aborigine population became broken up and reduced to slavery.

Ayers Rock

When was the sea bed explored?

In 1925 after having explored the mysteries of the jungle, the naturalized American **Charles William Beebe** turned his attention towards the **unknown sea bed**. He made the first tentative dives using only a basic **copper diving helmet** which enabled him to descend only a few metres in depth. In 1930, Beebe collaborated with **Otis Barton**, a young American inventor who, in his office in New Jersey, built the **Bathysphere**. On 6 June 1930, the two descended in the Bathysphere down into the **Bermuda Trench** at 250 metres depth. On 15 August 1934, they beat their former **record**, reaching **923 metres**, again using the wonderful Bathysphere.

Sea bed

WHAT IS THE BATHYSPHERE?

The Bathysphere (in the photograph, right) is a **steel capsule** in the **form of a sphere** and with a thickness of four centimetres.

It is equipped with a porthole made of quartz which is resistant to high pressures and is connected to the support ship by a strong steel cable.

During their dive, Beebe and Barton were hermetically sealed from the outside, to overcome the danger of water entering inside the capsule.

The supply of oxygen was regulated manually by Barton.

WHO BEAT ALL THE RECORDS FOR DESCENT?

On 23 January 1960 **Jacques Picard** *and* **Don Walsh** *descended with the* **bathyscaphe Trieste** *to the* **Marianne Trench**, *the largest sea trench in the Pacific Ocean, at a depth of* **10,911 metres**. *This incredible descent lasted 4 hours and 48 minutes and the two marine explorers remained on the sea bed for about half an hour before rising up in triumph.*

When was the North Pole reached for the first time?

Edwin Robert Peary

On 6 April 1909, **Edwin Robert Peary**, explorer and engineer in the American Navy, reached the **North Pole** accompanied by his friend **Matthew Henson** and four close Eskimo (Inuit) companions, **Ooquea**, **Ootah**, **Egingwah** and **Seegloo** whom they got to know during their long stay in the glacial Arctic Sea.

WHAT DID EDWIN ROBERT PEARY WEAR?
He wore Inuit dress, consisting of head covering, gauntlets and boots made of sealskin and seal fur.

The explorer Roald Engelbert Amundsen photographing the Norwegian flag after having reached the South Pole

AND THE SOUTH POLE?

Because of the harsh weather conditions, with gusts of winds more than 100 kilometres an hour and temperatures below -40°C, expeditions to the South Pole have caused the most interest. Norwegian explorer **Roald Engelbert Amundsen** sailed on the ship Fram to the South Pole in 1911. After landing in the Bay of Whales near the Ross Barrier and making base camp, he launched his expedition on 20 October. The expedition consisted of four men – **Oscar Wisting**, **Olav Bjaaland**, **Svere Hassel** and **Helmer Hansen**, each man on a sledge collectively pulled by **52 Husky dogs**. After almost two months of continuous travel, on 14 December, the explorers **finally arrived at the South Pole**. As a sign of their conquest, they planted the Norwegian flag. About one month after Amundsen, on 17 January 1912, the expedition led by the English explorer Robert Scott also reached the South Pole, by a different route. But the undertaking ended tragically with the death of all the team during the return journey.

EXCUSE ME, WHAT IS THE TIME?

If you were to find yourself at the North Pole and asked the time, prepare for a strange answer. 'What is that?' a person might say. **'Here, time does not exist**.*' At the North Pole, in fact, time is impossible to calculate, because the* **longitudes** *(the imaginary lines which divide the Earth lengthways)* **meet there.**

Igloo in Alaska

WHY DO WE NEED TO TREAT THE SOUTH POLE WITH RESPECT?

Because the South Pole represents **90% of the reserves of fresh water** of our entire planet.

CAN PEOPLE LIVE AT THE SOUTH POLE?

No, because the living conditions are too difficult. The Antarctic is the coldest continent (during the winter, temperatures plunge to **-60°C**, when it is also more windy and more dry). For explorers it is necessary to keep gloves on, even when blowing their nose, otherwise the mucus will freeze on the hand!

WHO LIVES AT THE NORTH POLE?

The Inuits, or 'true men' have settled even in eastern Siberia, in Greenland, Alaska and Canada. There are about 100,000 and they inhabit a **territory** called **Nunavut.**

Inuit Village

Who were the first to conquer Everest?

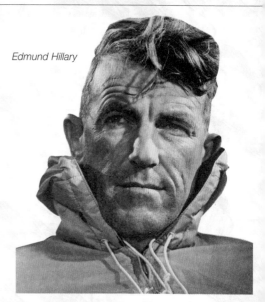
Edmund Hillary

Mount Everest was climbed for the first time in 1953 by the New Zealand mountaineer **Sir Edmund Hillary** and his **Nepalese Sherpa, Tenzing Norgay**. The two took part in an expedition led by English Colonel John Hunt and reached the '**roof of the world**' (8849.86 metres) at **11.30 on the morning of the 29 May**.

WHO ARE THE SHERPAS?

The Sherpas are a Nepalese people who live at high altitudes and who act as guides for mountaineers and carry their equipment on expeditions in the Himalya mountains.
They can bear the high altitudes without problems because their **blood is rich in haeomoglobin**, a pigment in the red blood corpuscles which carry oxygen from the lungs to the body tissues.

Nepalese Sherpa guides prepare for an expedition

NOT ONLY MEN
On 16 May 1975, **Junko Tabei**, *a 35 year old Japanese teacher became the* **first woman** *to climb Everest in an expedition of female mountaineers.*

WHAT IS THE NAME FOR EVEREST IN NEPALESE AND TIBETAN?
Everest in Nepalese is called **Sagarmatha** *('High in the Sky') and in Tibetan* **Chomo Lungma** *('Mother God of the Earth').*

ONCE AT THE TOP...

After having reached the summit of Everest, Tenzing Norgay buried biscuits and sweets in the snow to thank Buddha for his achievement. Edmund Hillary immortalized the historical moment by taking historic photographs...

Edmund Hillary and Tenzing Norgay sip tea after their conquest of the summit

A MEMORABLE JOURNEY

Fifty years later, **Peter Hillary** and **Jamling Tenzing Norgay** (sons of the first conquerors of Everest) celebrated the achievement of their fathers with an expedition financed by the National Geographic Expeditions Council. The expedition which tracked the same paths of descent as the two pioneers, took them over two months. The 84 year old Edmund Hillary was there to celebrate the undertaking, but without his faithful companion Tenzing Norgay who died in 1986.

WITHOUT OXYGEN CYLINDERS AND ALL ALONE

In August 1980, the mountaineer **Reinhold Messner** achieved a truly legendary undertaking: he climbed the roof of the world solo, and **without the aid of oxygen cylinders or radio**. Another truly impressive achievement was that of the Slovenik **Davo Karnicar** (7 October 2000) who, after reaching the summit, descended to base camp, climbing down for five hours uninterrupted. In May 2001 the very young **Marco Siffredi** challenged Everest, descending from the summit by snowboard. However, the following year, trying to repeat this descent, he disappeared tragically and his body has never been recovered.

WHO WAS EVEREST?

Sir George Everest *(1790-1866) was a mathematician, Governor General of India and Director General of the* **Survey of India***, a work full of observations and detail about the mountains of India. In 1852, after many surveys, it was discovered that a mountain called until then Peak XV was the highest in the world. It was decided to call this mountain Everest in his honour.*

The mountain chain of the Himalayas

When were the continents formed?

250 million years ago there existed just one continent called the **Pangea** (a word of Greek origin, meaning 'all the earth') surrounded by one ocean called **Panthalassa** ('all the seas' in Greek). Around 150 million years ago, the Pangea divided up and formed two continents: the **Laurasia** a land-mass of the continents which later became North America, Europe, Asia and Greenland, and the **Gondwana**, a land-mass of the continents south of the equator (Africa, South America, India, Australia and the Antarctic). The Panthalassa then underwent its own separation and from the one ocean was born the Atlantic and the Pacific. Laurasia and Gondwana, about 100 million years ago, divided to create continents which were smaller and very similar to those we know today: Africa separated from South America, and Australia became separated from the Antarctic.

*The Pangea as it must have looked at the end of the Paleozoic Era. The encroachment of the giant ocean **Tethys** made space for the formation of the Mediterranean Sea.*

The separation of a continental land-mass to the north would separate again into the North American and Euro-Asian continents.

WHAT WILL HAPPEN IN ANOTHER 50 MILLION YEARS?

The continents are always moving, **drifting**, so that the geographical theory is that Africa will reach Europe. This will lead to the shrinking of the Mediterranean Sea which will become a small lake, causing Sicily, Sardinia and Corsica to become closer together. Australia will move towards Asia, India will push ever more towards the continent of Asia and the Americas from the north to the south will move west, bringing about the expansion of the Atlantic Ocean.

Tsunami, tornados, earthquakes and volcanic eruptions form part of the natural life of the Earth.

ANIMALS
and
PLANTS

When did zoology begin?

Zoology is the study which classifies and studies all that is known about the animal world. It began many centuries ago with the work of the Greek philosopher **Aristotle** (384-322 BC). In his book *History of Animals, Parts of Animals* and *Generations of Animals*, he observed and described about 500 animals in great detail. After him, an important figure was the Latin scholar **Pliny the Elder** (23-79 BC) who dedicated much of his life to the study of zoology. His work *Historia naturalis* contained many excellent observations about animal life – but also much inaccurate information which was based on myth and legend.

Aristotle

Carl Linnaeus

Throughout the Middle Ages the works of Aristotle continued to form the basis of Zoology. Only in 1735 did it begin to develop on new lines, with the work of the Swedish naturalist **Carl Linnaeus** (1707-1778). In his book *Systema naturae*, Linnaeus sets out the first Table which defines classifications of all animals and plants. In the Linnaeus Table, each animal and plant is given a 'common name' and a scientific name in Latin, made up of two parts: the first part begins with a capital letter and indicates the genus, the second begins with a lower-case letter, and indicates its species. For example, the tiger in the Linnaeus Table is called *Panthera tigris* – that is, an animal of the genus panther and of the species tiger. Different genuses make up an order (e.g. carnivores) and two or more orders make up a class (e.g. mammals). In turn, all classes belong to a larger category which is called a **phylum** or 'type'. The largest phylum of all invertebrates – that is, among animals without a back-bone – is that of the arthropods, which has about 900,000 species. Of all vertebrates (animals with a back-bone) the largest phylum is fish with 25,000 known species.

THE NAME OF AN OSCAR...

Some years ago, a fossil of the Jurassic period was given a very strange name – **Jurassosaurus nedegoapeferkimorum**. *This name was made up from the initials of the names of actors in the film 'Jurassic Park'.*

WHAT ARE THE BESTIARES?

These are books about animals which were written in the Middle Ages. By today's standards, they are of little scientific value – but they are interesting because of the descriptions and legendary fantasies of many species. For example, it was thought that mice were born from dirty bread...

Who founded the first museum of natural history?

On 24 May 1683, in Oxford, England, **Elias Ashmole** opened the door of a public museum, which he called the Ashmolean. Inside an important private collection was exhibited. This collection had been received as a donation from the English botanical artist **John Tradescant** and his **son**. This collection was composed of many rare botanical exhibits and curious objects which Tradescant had discovered during his travels – unknown species of tropical plants, fossils, precious stones, pipes belonging to North American Indians, sacred relics, miniatures, rarities, coins and even salamanders and chameleons, all of which at that particular time would be classed as truly 'amazing'.

Fossil of a Trilobite

The pieces in the collection were catalogued and classified under the care of **Doctor Plot**, who was the first curator of the museum. The Ashmolean museum also housed a chemical laboratory equipped for experiments and teaching and some lecture rooms where university lessons were discussed.

During the 18th century, the museum suffered a period of neglect and many examples were lost, due to the poor conditions under which they were kept. But in the first half of the 19th century, the Ashmolean underwent a new development, thanks to the painstaking work of **brothers John and Philip Duncan** who re-classified exhibits and acquired new ones. After that, the **University of Oxford** decided to open a new museum of natural science to which they transferred many pieces from the collection at the Ashmolean. The museum of Elias Ashmole still survives, but now it specializes in archaeology.

WHAT IS THE ORIGIN OF THE WORD 'MUSEUM'?

Museum comes from the Greek word *Mousêion*, which can be translated as a 'place sacred to the Muses'. The original Museum was a building in the city of Alexandria in Egypt. Here there was a famous library where notable scholars met to talk together and to study.

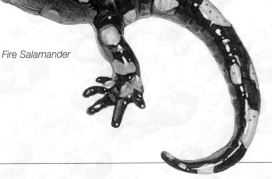

Fire Salamander

Who first studied the fossils of dinosaurs?

Mosasaurus, gigantic marine lizard

French naturalist **Georges Cuvier** (1769-1832) was the first to study and to reconstruct dinosaurs in detail. Thanks to him, a new scientific discipline, **palaeontology**, was born. As an expert at that time, Cuvier was often consulted to provide an opinion on the nature and the discovery of many fossils. One famous case was that of an enormous jaw of a marine lizard. Discovered in 1770 in Holland, this had been an object of controversy and discussion among scientists, until Cuvier established that it was the jaw-bone of a *Mosasaurus*. In 1796 he carried out an analysis of the remains found beneath the frozen ground of Siberia. These proved to be the remains of a prehistoric elephant, the **Mammoth**. But Cuvier's most sensational scientific discovery was the identification of a prehistoric reptile which he called **Pterodactyl**. Cuvier's studies came to the attention of a group of scientists, including **Richard Owen**, **Edward Cope**, and **Othniel Charles Marsh**. In 1841 it was Owen who invented the term 'dinosaur', meaning 'terrible lizard'. Cope was a great researcher into dinosaurs and discovered the *Camarasaurus* and the *Coelophysis*. Marsh, Professor of Palaeontology at Yale University, classified many fossils in great detail and discovered the *Stegosaurus* and the *Allosaurus*. Cope and Marsh were also fierce rivals: both gathered armed gangs together, ready to purloin fossil remains from the laboratories of the 'enemy'!

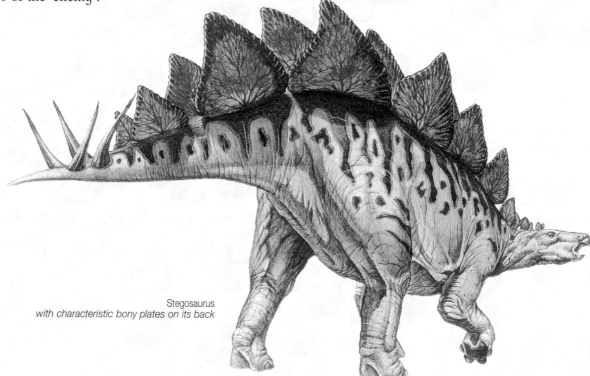

Stegosaurus with characteristic bony plates on its back

When did the first mammals apppear?

Cynognathus; *from which the first mammals descended*

Mammals first appeared more than 200 million years ago, in the **Triassic Period**, when the Earth was inhabited by dinosaurs. To begin with, living alongside dinosaurs was exhausting and extremely dangerous for them. The smaller mammals were often easy prey for dinosaurs and it was only due to their intelligence that they survived. Thanks to their small size and incredible agility, the first mammals succeeded in running to safety quickly, finding refuge in places inaccessible to the thick-skinned dinosaurs. The body of a mammal had a constant temperature (we call this 'warm-blooded') and so they could endure any sudden variation in the climate of the Earth without too much difficulty, whereas such conditions were deadly for some species of dinosaur. Also, a mammal's body was covered with hair and made waterproof by a layer of grease which insulated the body from cold and from heat. In addition, mammals had a maternal instinct, so that they took care of their young, whilst dinosaurs did not look after their eggs once they had been laid. But the main difference was the ability of the mother mammal to feed her young with food from her body. The first example of a mammal was the *Morganucodon* which lived 160 million years ago. It seems to have been similar to the shrew that we know today, feeding on insects and small animals.

Dimetrodon *with a large 'sail' on its back*

WHERE HAVE MAMMALS DESCENDED FROM?

From the family *Cinodonti*, a group of animals defined as reptile-mammals – reptiles similar to mammals, such as *Dimetrodon*, *Lycaenops* and *Massetognathus*.

The shrew is always hungry for insects

WHAT IS MAMMALOGY?
It is the branch of zoology which studies mammals.

When did dinosaurs become extinct?

Scaphognathus

Dinosaurs suddenly disappeared about 65 million years ago, at the end of the **Cretaceous** period. Until that time, these great reptiles had flourished for about 180 million years. But something disturbed the balance of the planet. Scientists have put forward many theories as to the reason for their extinction. The theory most widely-believed was that an enormous **asteroid** with a diameter between 10 to 14 kilometres, fell to the surface of the Earth about 65 million years ago. The impact would have caused a chain of disasters, including sea-quakes and a sudden drop in temperatures. Following such catastrophes, the dinosaurs disappeared for ever, leaving the way for a new species of animal, the **mammals**.

In February 2000, the space-craft **Space Shuttle Discovery** captured images which were relayed back to **NASA (National Aeronautics and Space Administration)** which confirmed the theory of the asteroid. These images showed the existence of an enormous crater with a diameter of 180 kilometres and 900 metres deep, in Yucatán, (Central America) and which originated from the fall of a heavenly body.

Tyrannosaurus

Diplodocus

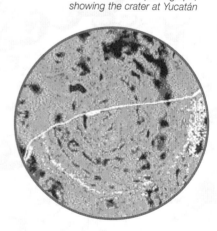

An infra-red satellite photograph, showing the crater at Yucatán

WHEN DID DINOSAURS LIVE?

Dinosaurs lived on Earth during the Mesozoic Era, between 245 and 65 million years ago. This was called the reptile age, because these animals were absolutely dominant.

TRUE GIANTS...

To begin with, the average length of a dinosaur varied between 2 and 5 metres. During the course of their evolution, many dinosaurs developed into gigantic creatures. **Sauropods** reached 50 metres in length. The enormous growth was probably due to the warm climate during the **Jurassic** period. Then the Earth was rich in lush vegetation and the larger dinosaurs got used to stretching their necks to reach the leaves on trees, without having to compete for food with smaller species.

CHAMPIONS OF SPEED

The fastest dinosaur was the **Ornithomimid**, which was similar to today's ostrich. This was a carnivore (meat-eater) with two very long, slender rear legs and which could probably reach speeds of 70 kilometres per hour. The slowest species were the herbivore (plant-eating) dinosaurs, such as the **Stegosaurus** which at maximum could only reach 6 kilometres per hour.

Iguanodon

CANNIBAL DINOSAURS

The dinosaur **Majungatholus atopus** was a fearsome predator, 9 metres in length. It lived about 80 million years ago in Madagascar and most probably ate others of its own kind. A group of paleontologists have found on this African island remains of fossilized bones with definite signs of chewing caused by a dinosaur of the same species.

Did you know...

It seems that the Sauropod dinosaurs could release great quantities of liquid, possibly urine. This discovery was announced during the 62nd Congress of American Society of the Paleontology of Vertebrates; researchers Katherine McCarville and Gale Bishop came to this conclusion after discovering a crater uncovered in the suburbs of the city of La Junta in Colorado, a zone famous for the numerous fossil remains and dinosaur footprints that have been found. According to the calculations of these two researchers, the small depression was just 30 centimetres deep, and could only have been caused by a jet of about 200 litres of liquid from a height of 2 metres – hence the theory that this was made by a dinosaur while passing urine.

What were mammoths?

A mammoth is killed by prehistoric hunters

Mammoths are the 'cousins' of elephants. Their scientific name *Elephas primigenius* points to their relationship.

Mammoths lived in Europe and North America during the Ice Age of the **Quaternary Period**, during the **Cenozoic Era**, from about 100,000 – 40,000 years ago. These gigantic, heavy monsters originated from Africa, and as they developed, so they adapted to life in very harsh climates.

A mammoth had two curved tusks, up to 4 metres long, which it used to scrape away the snow and uncover the plants on which it fed. Its body was covered with a thick wool, it weighed on average 4000 kilos and could reach a height of 4 metres. Mammoths became extinct 10,000 years ago. Many remains, perfectly preserved and including soft body parts as well as skeletons, have been discovered buried in the ice of Siberia and Alaska.

MAMMOTH NEW YORKERS!

As well as the cold zones of Europe and America, Mammoths also lived in the area which we know today as New York city.

MAMMOTHS LIKE BRICKS

Palaeolithic Man (600,000-10,000 years ago) used the bones of mammoth to build a framework structure for a hut. Some remains of these have been found in the Ukraine.

WHEN WAS THE FIRST MAMMOTH DISCOVERED?

It was discovered in 1900 on the banks of the River Beresovka in Siberia. Dogs belonging to fur-hunters sniffed out the body of a mammoth, still partly covered by the ice.

When palaeontologists came on the scene, they found the skin, the fur and the blood of the animal, still perfectly preserved.

When did mammoths die out?

Mammoths disappeared a few thousand years ago. There are many theories on their extinction. The most likely of these theories attributes their disappearance to the changes in climate. In the **Pleistocene Era**, the first part of the **Quaternary Period** between 1,650,000 and 10,000 years ago, the Earth underwent sudden drops in temperature (in Europe, we know about four **Ice Ages**), with freezing conditions spreading from the edges of the glaciers even as far as the previously temperate zones of the northern prairies. The mammoths did not succeed in adapting themselves to the new climatic conditions and so they died out. Recent studies have shown the extraordinary coincidence between the appearance of humankind in the Pleistocene Era and the beginning of the decline of the mammoth. So, the theory is that the prehistoric hunters could have killed off the mammoth, causing its extinction, or that the first human beings carried a virus which was harmless to people, but proved deadly to the ancestors of the elephant.

Fossil of Lariosaurus

Fossil of Seymouria Baylareusis

Did you know...

Palaeontology is the science of the study of fossils – that is, all the animals and organisms which lived in prehistoric times.

How do beavers build their homes?

Beavers are rodent mammals which live on the banks of rivers and streams and spend a lot of their time in lairs which they build using straw and mud. This lair is semi-submerged and has one main living space above the level of the water, connected to an entrance, and a 'store-room' where the beaver keeps its reserves of food. Both the entrance and the store-room are underground. To get the material they need, beavers fell trees, nibbling around the base of tree-trunks and then gnawing the wood into different lengths. The beaver uses these pieces of wood, cemented together with the mud and stones, to build a dam around its lair to make it more safe. The dam creates a sort of lake around the beaver's home, where the level of water is always the same. In winter, when the surface of the water is frozen, beavers swim underwater to reach their food supplies.

IDENTITY OF A BEAVER

There are two main species of beavers with very similar characteristics. In Europe and Asia lives the **Castor fiber fiber** *('Old World' Beaver) whilst the* **Castor fiber canadensis** *('New World' Beaver) lives in America. Each has a stocky, squat body, with webbed rear feet and a flat tail, which it uses as a rudder when it swims, but which can also signal danger when the beaver smacks it down on the surface of the water. Beavers have incisor teeth covered with orange-coloured enamel. Its teeth are very strong, for the job of 'wood-cutting' which the beaver has to do to build its home!*

WHAT GIVES PINK FLAMINGOS THEIR COLOUR?

Flamingos are naturally pink, but the colour would soon fade without **carotene**, which is a natural pink pigment, or colouring. Carotene is found in shrimps, and so parks and zoos feed flamingos with as many shrimps as they like to eat.

WHY DOES THE ZEBRA HAVE STRIPES?

Stripes are very useful to the zebra. They help the animal to confuse the fierce lion which is always on the look-out for prey. The stripes makes it difficult for any animal hunting the zebra to distinguish clearly a whole herd of zebras on the move. According to some studies, the zebra's stripes constitute a sort of **identity profile** for each animal, because each one has a striped coat which is different to any other zebra. Also, the characteristic colours, white and black, help to regulate the body temperature.

Did you know...

In Africa, attempts have been made to tame wild zebras, to use them as load-bearing beasts, like camels. So far, these attempts have been successful! But the work has taken a lot of time and costs a great deal of money.

WHAT ARE 'HUMP-BACKS'?

These are the **camel** and the **dromedary**! For these animals, the hump is an important reserve of energy, a sort of portable 'pantry' which can weigh up to 35 kilos. Inside the hump are reserves of food and water, in the form of fat, and which is always ready when it is needed. In the desert, these animals can survive without eating or drinking, even for whole weeks. But when they reach an oasis, they need to renew their reserves of water. A dromedary can drink up to **135 litres of water** in only ten minutes!

A camel has two humps

A dromedary has one hump

Did you know...

Camels and dromedaries also live in Australia, where there are between 600 and 750 thousand. The first were imported by European explorers to be used as load-carrying beasts ('beasts of burden') and in the construction of the first trans-continental telegraph line.

How do birds fly?

Collared puff bird

Great spotted woodpecker

Birds fly by batting their wings, lifting them up and then lowering them. This action produces a strong thrust forward, and this thrust enables the bird to rise into the air. When it reaches a certain speed, the bird can then spread its wings and let itself be transported by the currents of air. When this happens, we say the bird is gliding, and this is the least tiring way of flying. The skeleton of a bird is solid, but light, and with strong pectoral (chest) muscles, all perfectly structured for flight. A bird's digestion is also very efficient. In just a few minutes, it transforms food into the energy necessary for the activity of flight. Its respiratory (breathing) system is always ready to supply exactly the right amount of oxygen which the bird needs, even to fly across great oceans.

How do insects flutter their wings?

Dragonfly

The complete movement of insects to fly is extremely complex. **The wings**, which beat at between 20 to 600 times per second, make a **similar movement** to the **blinking of an eyelid**, or the movement of an oar during a boat-race. When the wing is lowered, the front part turns upward; whilst when the wing lifts up, the rear part moves down.

Did you know...

A team of researchers at the University of Berkeley in California have built a mechanical fly which they call **Robofly** to study the movement of wings.

Anna's hummingbird

AERIAL ACROBATS WITH A VICE-LIKE GRIP

The tiny hummingbird originates from the tropical regions of America. It can fly forward, back, upside down and straight up, as well as hovering in the air. The beats of its wings are so fast and so frequent that the wings themselves become invisible. In the heat of the sun, the **hummingbird** chooses a branch on which to perch and go to sleep. Then, its claws sink into the branch and the bird's tendons contract instinctively. This 'automatic' action gives the hummingbird such a strong grip that it can remain fixed firmly and relaxed on the branch of the tree, not only throughout the night, but also in death.

Sparkling violet-ear hummingbird

A NON-FLYING BIRD

The penguin comes from the South Pole. It is a bird which cannot fly. In any case, its wings would be too weak to lift its heavy body and its big tummy off the ground. But the penguin is a wonderful diver and swimmer, able to cover 10 kilometres in one hour.

The **Emperor Penguin** can swim even faster, reaching speeds of 27 kilometres per hour.

The real reason for the penguin's inability to fly is because at the South Pole, the only source of food is in the sea. The entire Antarctic is completely covered by ice all the year round and so the penguin does not need to fly to get its food.

Penguins

Wilson's Petrel

Screaming albatross

WHY DO BIRDS FLY IN A 'V' SHAPE?

The 'V' formation is useful to birds in flight, due to **aerodynamics** (movement of bodies through a flow of air). In this formation, the birds can use the vortexes (whirls) and the push of the air which is created during flight. The only bird not to benefit from all this is the one which leads the way, and so is at the centre point of the 'V' shape. But all the birds take it in turns to be in this 'uncomfortable' position.

Anhinga

How do bees make honey?

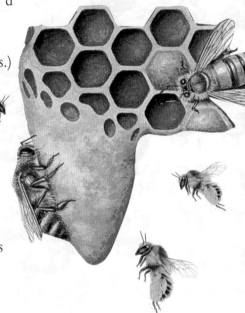

Honeybees are the bees that make honey. They live in a colony led by a Queen Bee. The Queen lays eggs which will hatch into worker bees (underdeveloped females), queens and males (or drones) whose job it is to fertilize the queens. (Later, these queens will form their own colonies.) Honeybees make honey with nectar (liquid sugar) and the pollen from flowers. During the summer, each worker bee uses its tongue, called a **glossa**, to suck nectar and pollen from the flowers, both of which it keeps in its stomach. When its stomach is full, all the bees return to the hive. Here, other worker bees are waiting to collect the liquid and mix it with secretions from their mouths, which they then deposit in the cells of the **honeycomb**. After three days, this substance is transformed into honey. The cells are then sealed with plugs of wax, so that the honey is kept safely, ready for the winter.

Did you know...

To fill a 450g jar of honey, ten honeybees would have to work all their lives.

BEES VERSUS HORNETS

From ancient times, hornets have been the enemies of bees. But bees have devised ways to kill them. The first way is by 'suffocation', where the bee covers the hornet with wax and poisons any hornet which has come into its hive.
The second method of killing is by 'burning alive'. When bees see the hornet, they surround it in the form of a ball and flap their wings all together at the same time. This movement produces heat, and after about four minutes, the temperature becomes unbearable. After 30 minutes, when the temperature can reach 46°, the poor hornet falls to the ground, roasted.

WHAT IS A HONEYCOMB?

A honeycomb is made up of the little cells of wax made by the worker bees, all joined up together. Each cell is hexagonal (six-sided) in shape, which means that no wax and no space is wasted – because each side of each cell joins up perfectly with each cell next to it on all sides.

BEES ANTI-TERRORIST MISSION

In the laboratories of the Pentagon in Washington, unusual experiments have been carried out with bees. Scientists have been trying to 'transform' bees into unsuspicious 'spies' against terrorist attacks. Entire colonies of bees have been trained to prefer the smell of explosives to the scent of flowers. The results of a three-year study show that bees possess a well-developed and highly sensitive sense of smell, very similar to that of dogs. So far, these trials have had positive results, and tests have proved that hidden explosives have been discovered in 99% of cases.

Succinea

How can we recognize a snail?

The name 'snail' can apply to many species of small-size molluscs, where a body is contained within a spiral shell. At the head of the snail there are four appendages (two longer than the other two), with **tentacles** which the snail can stretch out and retract the moment they come in contact with anything. These 'horns' are the sense organs with which the snail can touch and sense the smallest of objects. At the ends of the longest appendages there are dark-coloured points. These are the ends of the snail's eyes, and these are contained within little canals which can move up and down. In the event of danger, the snail can withdraw these eyes back inside its head.

Achatina fulica

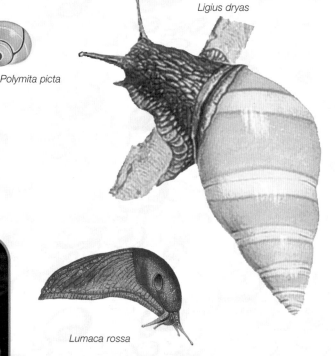

Ligius dryas

Polymita picta

A PROTECTIVE SHELL
The shell of a snail acts as the perfect shelter during hibernation and when conditions outside the shell are particularly dangerous or harsh. In either case, the body retreats inside and the snail secretes a substance which closes the opening of the shell, but allows air to filter through.

Lumaca rossa

NIGHT-TIME VEGETARIANS!
The snail spends much of each day simply hiding inside its shell. It is at night time that it goes in search of food. It feeds on plant material, preferring plants with plenty of leaves. For this reason, the snail is regarded as a pest because of the damage it can do to growing crops and flowers. However, there are some species which are specially bred for eating as a great delicacy.

common lizard

Two lizards 'settling a score'

HOW LONG DOES A LIZARD LIVE?

The **common lizard** can live up to ten years. The tail of the lizard can grow back up to four times.

HOW LONG DOES A MUSSEL LIVE?

The average life of this mussel, which lives on plankton, is about four years.

Pearl Oyster

dog ticks

HOW LONG DOES A TICK LIVE?

The life cycle of a **tick** can be within a period of time from two months to two years. The average life of a tick is one year. It feeds on blood.

WHICH IS THE CREATURE WITH THE MOST EYES?

The **dragonfly** has about 28,000 eyes. Second place goes to the **fly** with 4,000 eyes! Lucky for them that they never need to see an optician!

HOW LONG DOES A FLY LIVE?

The life of an adult fly is about three weeks, during which time it feeds on liquid sugar from plants or on the food of animals.

Two dragonflies photographed at different stages of their lives

SEPARATED BY ICE

The **penguin** and the **polar bear** are the two most famous mammals of icy regions – but they never meet. Why? Because **penguins** live at the South Pole and **polar bears** live at the North Pole.

Where does the giant squid live?

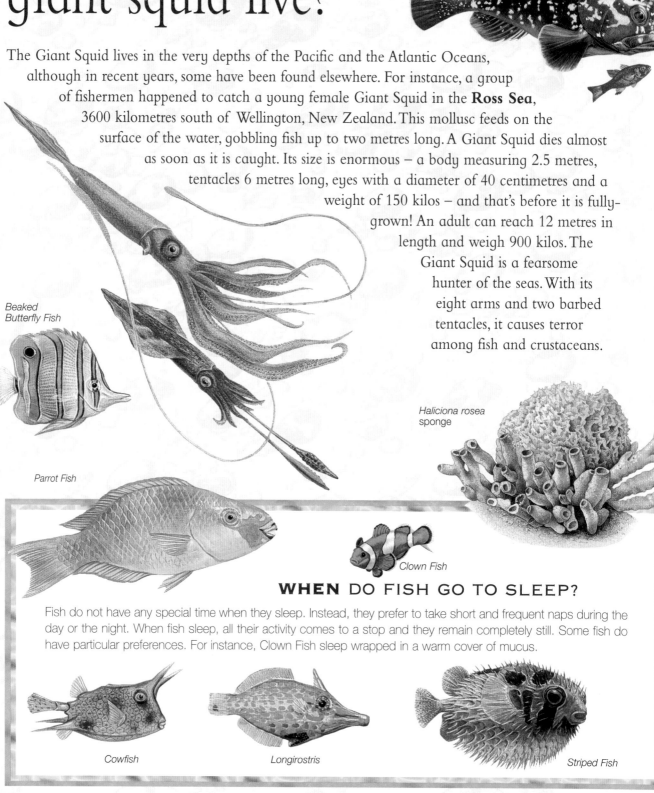

Grouper

The Giant Squid lives in the very depths of the Pacific and the Atlantic Oceans, although in recent years, some have been found elsewhere. For instance, a group of fishermen happened to catch a young female Giant Squid in the **Ross Sea**, 3600 kilometres south of Wellington, New Zealand. This mollusc feeds on the surface of the water, gobbling fish up to two metres long. A Giant Squid dies almost as soon as it is caught. Its size is enormous – a body measuring 2.5 metres, tentacles 6 metres long, eyes with a diameter of 40 centimetres and a weight of 150 kilos – and that's before it is fully-grown! An adult can reach 12 metres in length and weigh 900 kilos. The Giant Squid is a fearsome hunter of the seas. With its eight arms and two barbed tentacles, it causes terror among fish and crustaceans.

Beaked Butterfly Fish

Haliciona rosea sponge

Parrot Fish

Clown Fish

WHEN DO FISH GO TO SLEEP?

Fish do not have any special time when they sleep. Instead, they prefer to take short and frequent naps during the day or the night. When fish sleep, all their activity comes to a stop and they remain completely still. Some fish do have particular preferences. For instance, Clown Fish sleep wrapped in a warm cover of mucus.

Cowfish

Longirostris

Striped Fish

Do fish detect smells?

Siamese Fighting Fish

Surgeon Fish

In fish, smell is the most highly-developed sense. Most of all, smell helps fish in their search for food. The **eel** can detect smells up to a distance of 50 metres! But smell is also important in mating. At mating-time, the female releases a substance called **pheromone** into the water and this has a smell that attracts the male as a signal that the female is ready to be fertilized. Their sense of smell also enables fish to detect and to escape from predators. Finally, its sense of smell helps fish to find their way around vast oceans. **Salmon** have a 'smell memory' which enables them to recognize the way home, when they leave the ocean to swim up the rivers and back to the places where they were born.

Red Salmon

Common Torpedo

Eel

Bunodactis verrucoso

Did you know...

The **Starfish** has many eyes positioned at the points of its five arms.

HOW DO PELICANS FISH UNDER WATER?

Pelicans cannot see under water. That is why they have to recognize their prey from up high and then dive under to catch it.

Who first made use of rubber trees?

The first people to make use of rubber trees were the North American Indians. They taught themselves how to use latex, a substance extracted from the bark of the tree *Hevea brasiliensis*, better known as the **Rubber Tree**, and how to obtain rubber (or India rubber) after the process of '**coagulation**' or '**clotting**'. This new material reached Europe following the discovery of America. **Christopher Columbus** returned from his legendary voyage bringing with him a mysterious product of India rubber – a rubber ball.

The first person to set out scientific facts about the Rubber Tree was the French physicist **Charles-Marie de la Condamine**. In 1736, after completing a journey in South America he demonstrated the valuable qualities of India rubber to the French Academy. But quite a few years were to elapse before rubber became both useful and important.

In 1839, the USA inventor **Charles Goodyear** developed the process of **vulcanization**, a method by which rubber became stronger and more flexible. After this discovery, rubber began to be used in many fields. In 1898, Goodyear founded the company which became the major manufacturer of pneumatic tyres, Goodyear.

Pneumatic tyres

Did You Know...

The natives of South America extracted the sap from the Rubber Tree and used it in a way which is still well-known to us. They made large balls to play with. The native word 'caoutchouc' can be translated as 'the tree which cries'.

Extracting the latex

How do bananas reproduce?

Bananas belong to a group of plants which reproduce without seeds. Instead, the shoots of a new plant grow from a **rhizome**, an underground stem which develops horizontally, similar to a tuber or a bulb. These underground stems take nutriments from the soil and store substances which are necessary for the growth of the new shoots. But just to clear up any confusion – **the banana is not a tree. It is a gigantic herb**, up to 9 metres high and which grows rapidly from the underground stem within about one year, to produce fruit and then dies. The banana is the fleshy fruit of this plant and was known in ancient times. We know that it was first eaten 10,000 years ago. The Greeks, the Romans and the Arabs also knew and ate the banana. The fruit came from southern Asia and was exported to the New World only after 1500. Since then, its cultivation spread and it is now grown in many countries throughout the world. The banana exists in many varieties and also in many different colours. In countries such as Asia and Africa the banana is an important food in everyday diet. However, its survival is seriously threatened by a disease the *Panama disease*, and by parasites which infest the little plants.

WHAT IS THE SCIENTIFIC SOLUTION?

To ward off the danger and to save the banana from possible extinction, scientists have proposed finding and then reading and de-coding its DNA (molecular structure). With this, it may be possible to create an artificial species of banana which is resistant to disease.

What is the longest-living plant?

The coconut palm, **Cocos nucifera**, is a plant which can live up to 100 years. It grows along the African coasts and in all tropical zones, especially along the coast, where the ground is sandy. It is sometimes called the **queen of vegetables** because of the quantity of fruit which it yields. Its fruit, the coconut, is not only nutritious, it also contains a liquid sugar, coconut milk, which can be drunk and enjoyed as well as being used in the finest and most refreshing cocktail drinks. Oil can be extracted from the pulp of the coconut, the **copra**, to make soap and candles, flour and cooking fats (coconut oil is used in the manufacture of margarine). Its leaves are used to make baskets, rush-matting and ropes. From the shell can be made unusual buttons and rings.

Coconuts

Sacred Baboon

Male macaque

The long-tailed macaque is one of the most beautiful of macaques

WHAT IS THE ORIGIN OF NAME COCOS NUCIFERA?

The name *cocos* comes from a Portuguese word, macaco, which means monkey. The reason for this name may be because of three holes of germination in the **endocarp**, the innermost layer of the fruit – two are closed and one is open, similar to the mouth of a monkey.

Nucifera is from the Latin, and is a name made up of *nuci*, meaning 'nuts' and *fero* a latin verb which means to bear or to carry. And so the meaning of *nucifera* is therefore 'carrier of nuts'.

Where does the chocolate bean grow?

Cacao plant

The **cacao tree** comes from the woody, hot, humid zones of South America. Its cultivation has spread to western Africa, through the work of French and English settlers. Today, Africa has become the major world producer of the chocolate bean. Its 'discoverer' was the Spanish conqueror of Peru, **Hernán Cortés** (1485-1547). He was the first to see the **Aztecs** using the bean of the cacao tree and brought three cases of chocolate beans back to Europe.

The first product of the cacao appreciated by the Europeans was **cocoa**. The chocolate bar did not appear until the beginning of the 1800s and milk chocolate was not made until 1876.

The **Aztecs** sweetened the taste of the chocolate bean by mixing it with honey and sugar cane or maize. They also used chocolate beans in exchange for goods; the life of a rabbit was worth only ten cacao seeds!

When did coffee come to Europe?

The coffee plant is part of the rubiaceae family

Coffee reached Europe, or more precisely, Venice, in about 1590. The drink originated in regions near the Red Sea, and the first people to savour the quality and the aroma were Arab merchants who journeyed from the Middle East. Thanks to these **Arabs**, coffee began to be drunk in many European countries within a few centuries. The cultivation of coffee was also exported and introduced into tropical zones of South America. Today, the major producers of coffee are Brazil, Vietnam and Columbia.

How can we tell the age of a tree?

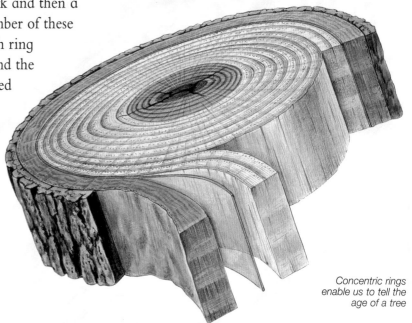

If we were to cut the trunk of a tree into horizontal slices, we would see on the outside a layer of bark and then a series of **concentric rings**. Count the number of these rings – and that is the age of the tree. Each ring corresponds to one year in the tree's life, and the space between one ring and the next is filled with a layer of soft wood which the tree produced within the space of 12 months. From the thickness of this wood, we can tell if that year was dry or rainy; if a ring is thin, that means the tree had drunk little during that year. If a ring is wide, then the tree enjoyed a year of plenty.

Concentric rings enable us to tell the age of a tree

Baobab

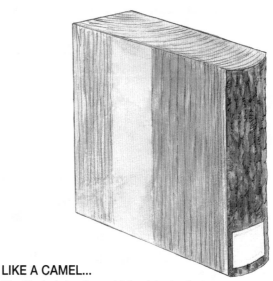

LIKE A CAMEL...
The Baobab is a tree which originates from tropical Africa. It has a remarkable capacity for absorbing water – up to 1000 litres per day!

How does a petrified forest form?

Section of a fossilized tree-trunk

A petrified forest originated during the course of many geological events, as a consequence of volcanic eruptions, fires and earthquakes. It is made of **fossilized remains** in which the **atoms of silicone** have replaced all the hard parts of the trees, and so their structure is perfectly preserved. This process is called **silicization** and it has the effect of giving the trees a 'petrified' or stone-like appearance.

In Anglona region of the island of Sardinia, there is a petrified forest which was formed about 20 million years ago. Following a tremendous volcanic eruption, the entire zone was covered with a layer of cinders rich in silicone and which fossilized the trees.

The Petrified Forest National Park, Arizona

When do trees lose their leaves?

Trees lose their leaves in the autumn, of course! Broad-leaved trees, such as elm, willow and oak, shed their leaves as a defence against the winter cold. If their leaves did not fall, they would take so much energy and water from the tree, more than could be absorbed by the roots. Apart from this, it is best for the tree if leaves are renewed each year. These trees are called **deciduous**. **Aghiform trees** (such as pine and spruce) with needle-shaped leaves, shed their leaves a little at a time throughout the year. These trees are called **evergreen**.

WHAT IS PHOTOSYNTHESIS?

This is an important **biological process** through which green plants are able to get the necessary nutriments. Photosynthesis takes place due to chlorophyll, a green pigment found in the surface layer of each leaf, which captures energy from the sun and transforms this into chemical energy. Thanks to this chemical energy, **carbon dioxide** is absorbed from the air and transformed by the plant into **sugar**, which it needs in order to live. This chemical process also releases **oxygen** – and so photosynthesis is essential for us human beings, as well as plants.

Pine cone, 'fruit' of the conifer

WHEN CAN TREES CAUSE DAMAGE?
In Madagascar, the deforestation and methods of cultivation in the wild has ruined 75 – 90% of the land.

Oak tree

How do plants without flowers reproduce?

Ferns, mosses, horsetails and algae reproduce by **spores**. These are microscopic cells capable of **agamic** (non-sexual) **reproduction** and which drop from the plant to begin a new life. Each spore can produce at least one new plant. Conifers (cypress, pine and fir trees) reproduce by the seeds contained within their cones. All plants in this family (gymnosperm) have separate male and female sex organs. Inside the female cones are the ovaries, ready to be fertilized by pollen produced within the male cones and carried by the wind. From this fertilization comes new seeds.

Algae

Mosses

WHEN DID FERNS AND HORSETAILS FIRST APPEAR?

Ferns and horsetails are **prehistoric plants**. They first appeared on Earth about 300 million years ago in the **carboniferous period**. Together, these plants formed the major part of the vegetation on Earth and were the favourite foods of plant-eating dinosaurs. Entire forests of horsetails, up to 18 metres high, grew undisturbed, whilst today, we can count only 30 species. So, horsetails can be regarded as surviving fossils! By contrast, ferns have survived more successfully, and today there are about 10,000 species.

Where do the tallest trees in the world grow?

Giant Sequoia

The tallest trees in the world are to be found in California, USA, in the mountains of **Sierra Nevada**. In protected National Parks, such as the **Sequoia National Park**, there are Sequoia trees (sometimes known as the 'patriarchs' or ancestors of nature). These are true 'giants' with an average life of between 2200 and 4000 years! The highest of all is the **Mendocino Tree**, with a height of 117 metres, followed by the **General Sherman**, at 83 metres high and a trunk 11 metres in diameter.

Wood of sequoia trees in the National Sequoia Park, California

The 'old general', over 2200 years of age!

HOW WERE FORESTS OF FERNS TRANSFORMED?

The immense, prehistoric forests of ferns, up to 50 metres high, were transformed over the course of thousands of years into carbon fossil or fossilized carbon. Even today, the fossilized remains of ferns can be found perfectly preserved – in coal!

Sequoia

WHERE ARE THE RAINFORESTS?

Rainforests are in the equatorial, tropical regions of our planet. These forests are populated by over 50% of all species of animals and plants on Earth.

Ferns grow in humid places

WHERE IS THE OLDEST TREE ON EARTH?

The oldest tree on Earth is in the White Mountains, California, USA. It is called **Methuselah** and it is a pine tree with an estimated age of 4747 years. Its needles remain attached to its branches for 20 years before falling to the ground.

SCIENCE
and
TECHNOLOGY

Who said that humans are descended from monkeys?

Charles Robert Darwin (1809-1882) English biologist and naturalist proposed the theory of **natural evolution** (or 'Darwinism'). According to this theory, all living things, animals and plants, are subject to continual evolution (or development) and have evolved from common ancestors. According to Darwin, human beings have evolved from animals similar to monkeys. This process took place due to **natural selection** – only those who could adapt to their surroundings survived and through reproduction passed on to successive generations hereditary characteristics which made them even stronger. Darwin was the first to consider this natural selection in a positive way, as a strength which enables the species to progress. He formed his theory after having travelled around the world **aboard his ship, the Beagle** and visiting such places as Cape Verde, Patagonia, Tierra del Fuego, Brazil, Chile, Peru, the coral islands of the Indian Ocean and the Galapagos Islands.

Darwin's **expedition** lasted five years from 1831 until 1836. During this time he collected lots of information and observations on the fauna (wild life) and flowers of the places he visited. In 1859, Darwin published his most famous work, *The Origin of Species by Natural Selection.* The news that this book was being published aroused so much interest, that the first edition of 1000 copies was sold out in just one day.

Charles Robert Darwin

Frontispiece of the book 'The Origin of Species' 1859

Did you know...

As a boy, Darwin did not know what he wanted to do when he grew up. At first, he was interested in medicine, but he soon gave this up because he could not stand the sight of blood.

The Beagle in full sail

Who invented the infinity (never-ending) symbol?

In 1655, the English mathematician **John Wallis**, one of the most learned men of his age, concentrated on deciding what would be the infinite symbol. He chose the sign ∞, which is rather like the number 8 on its side, to indicate infinity. The reason for this choice was never clearly explained. One theory is that it was derived from the letter M which the Romans used to indicate the number one thousand.

A second explanation suggests that both the Roman M and the ∞ symbol are different graphic forms of the Greek letter f *(phi)*. The symbol was not accepted at first. **It only began to be used worldwide in 1800.**

The infinity (never-ending) symbol

zero صِفْرٌ جَ أَصْفَار

The word zero in Arabic is written like this

WHO INVENTED THE SIGN FOR ZERO?

The **zero** sign was officially introduced to western culture by the Arab mathematician **Muhammad ibn Musa al-Khwarizmi** who lived from about 780-800 AD. But the zero sign only began to be widely used two centuries later, through the efforts of a French monk **Gerbert of Aurillac** who later became Pope Sylvester II.

The symbol 0 comes from the Arabic '**sifr**' which means 'nothing' or 'nought'. The Italian mathematician **Leonardo Fibonacci** was the first to understand its importance in calculation and introduced it into Europe. In 1202 Fibonacci made known the Indo-Arabic sequence of numbers through his paper *Liber abaci* ('Book of the Abacus').

The first calculating device was invented in France in 1642 by Blaise Pascal. It could do subtractions and additions automatically.

Who was the pioneer of modern science?

From 1452 to 1519, at the heart of the Renaissance, there lived a multi-faceted genius – artist, sculptor, architect, water engineer, inventor – **Leonardo da Vinci**. da Vinci is widely regarded as the forerunner of modern science and there is no doubt that his observations on the natural world and the functions of machines put him ahead of his time. He spent much of his life observing nature and the human body, carrying out his first studies on anatomy on corpses which he obtained from hospitals. He was also fascinated by the flight of birds, as well as the flight of bats and the kite. From observing and studying the movement of wings, Leonardo designed and built **mechanical wings** with the idea of making it possible for **people to take to flight**. He also invented a glider with

The bombard

movable wings, similar to that of a bat and very similar to the glider used in prototype experiments 400 years later by the German engineer Otto Lilienthal.

da Vinci thought up hundreds of inventions, such as the **aerial screw** which introduced the **principle of the helicopter**, later used by engineer Enrico Forlanini in 1877 to build the first steam-powered helicopter, and a **weaving loom** operated by one weaver and two centuries ahead of the mechanical loom invented in 1733 by the Englishman John Kay. Leonardo da Vinci also designed a **motorised cart** – a forerunner of the motor car, the **ventilator**, the **parachute** (this project of Leonardo's was tested with great success by London artchitect Adrian Nicholas), the **lifejacket**, the **bicycle**... the list goes on.

The armoured wagon

da Vinci was also interested in the idea of machines for war and built a **covered armoured wagon**. This design was developed into the first tank and was used many centuries later during the First World War. He also designed the **bombard**, a weapon able to fire missiles repeatedly, rather like the modern-day mortar bomb, and devised **giant crossbows, multiple-barrelled machine guns** and many other machines of war, all of which were astonishing for the age in which he lived.

The scythe cart

The bicycle

da Vinci's flying machine

Did you know...

From the writings of Giorgio Vasari (Renaissance writer, artist and architect), it is known that Leonardo da Vinci was a strict vegetarian. He would even go to the market to buy tender, young chickens, not to kill and then cook them, but to set them free to fly away.

WHERE ARE THE DESIGNS AND PROJECTS OF LEONARDO KEPT?

On the death of Leonardo on 2 May 1519, in the castle of Cloux, in Amboise, France, all his manuscripts, studies and designs were inherited by his favourite pupil Francesco Melzi, who guarded them jealously until his own death in 1570. From that date, over 5000 pages of manuscripts passed from one person to another. At one time there were 40 'codices', files containing da Vinci's notebooks on different themes. Today, 21 codices have survived, including – *Codice Arundel, Codice Atlantic, Codice on the flight of birds, Codice Ashburnham, Codice of the French Institute, Codici Forster, Codice Leicester, Windsor Pages* and *Codice of Madrid*. Most of these are kept in institutes, museums and libraries in France, Italy, England and Spain. The one exception is the Codice Leicester, which is kept in the USA after having been acquired by **Bill Gates**, owner of Microsoft, for the 'modest' price of around 30 million American dollars.

Machine gun

WHY DID LEONARDO WRITE FROM RIGHT TO LEFT?

Leonardo was left-handed. So, contrary to what was usually done, he would not write on a sheet of paper from the left, because his sleeve would smudge the ink. Instead, he wrote from right to left.

Aerial screw

Who was the most prolific inventor in history?

Thomas Alva Edison (1847-1931) was an American inventor,who in his life registered **1093 patents**.He invented the **phonograph** (1876), **the electric light bulb** (1879) a type of early **duplicator**,the **mimeograph** for the reproduction of documents (1887), the **power station** (1882) the **cathode-ray tube** (1876) and he perfected the **telephone**.

Thomas Alva Edison

Telephone apparatus dating from the beginning of 1900

HOW MANY TELEPHONE CALLS ARE MADE EACH DAY?

There are about **13 billion telephone calls** made each day across the world – and Scandinavia is the region in which there are the greatest number of telephone lines per head. The advent of the cellular telephone has also increased the exchange of communication. For example, **each day** throughout the world about one billion text messages are sent, that is 11,500 every second.

HOW DOES THE TELEPHONE WORK?

The telephone works due to **sound waves**. Inside the telephone receiver mouthpiece, there is a **membrane** which vibrates when it is hit by sound waves emitted when a person talks. These vibrations are then transformed into **electric current** and pass through electric cables. When the electric current reaches its destination, it is transformed back into sound waves, enabling the person who is receiving the call to hear the voice at the other end of the telephone, even over a distance of thousands of kilometres.

The telephone was invented in 1871 by an Italian emigrant to the USA, **Antonio Meucci**, but the origin of his invention was hidden for many years. The truth was that Meucci did not have the necessary money to patent his invention. Instead, in**1876**, a patent was registered by **Alexander Graham Bell**. The whole matter became the subject of a long, legal dispute, which was won in 1887 by Bell, who took full commercial advantage of the invention. Meucci died in 1889, and it was only on **15 June 2002** that the **USA House of Representatives** attributed the invention of the telephone to him, bringing this long controversy to an end.

How does a lift work?

A lift (or elevator) comprises – a **cabin** to carry people or goods, an **electric motor**, a **motorized pulley**, an **electric cable**, and **counter-weights**, blocks of cast iron to balance the weight of the cabin. The cabin of the lift is raised by the electric cable. The electric motor works the pulley, which winds and unwinds the cable, so that the cabin ascends and descends. The cabin moves up and down the **lift shaft**.

The counter-weight prevents the electric motor from 'bouncing' the load in the cabin so that this can proceed smoothly.

Inside the lift, there is push-button panel to direct the lift and also to sound an alarm in the event of an emergency.

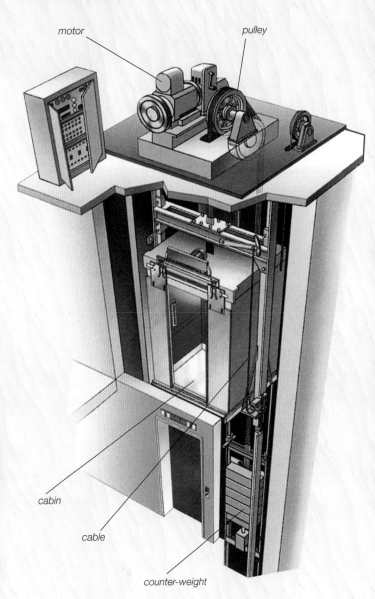

motor pulley

cabin

cable

counter-weight

WHEN WAS THE LIFT INVENTED?

Hydraulic lifts appeared in Europe at the beginning of the 1800s. But because they were not all that safe, they were used to carry goods for industrial use.

The first passenger safety lift was built on **23 March 1857 by the American Elisha Graves Otis** for the large stores Haughwout and Co. in Broadway, New York.

The **first-ever lifts appeared** in the third century BC and were used to carry the **gladiators** from the underground regions of the Colosseum in Rome, ready to take part in the violent 'games'. These lifts were operated manually, by slaves or by animals.

OTIS BEATS DEATH

Elisha Otis installed a security device in his passenger lift, to prevent the cabin falling if the cable broke. He demonstrated this himself, by riding on the platform up into the air, along with cases, barrels and other heavy objects, and then **ordering the cable which carried the lift to be cut**. The lift began to descend, but after a few seconds, the cabin stopped. The safety device had worked!

Who invented the microscope?

Electronic microscope

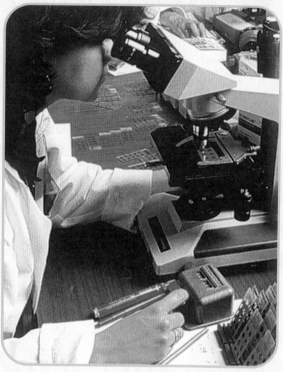

The invention of the microscope (from the Greek word *micros*, meaning small and *scopéo*, meaning observe) dates back to the first experiments with lenses, carried out in 1590 by two Dutch spectacle makers, **Hans and Zacharias Jansen**.

These two craftsmen made the first optical microscope, so-called because it had two lenses – the **objective**, which produced an enlarged image of an object, and the **ocular** which enlarged this image up to 30 times. The Dutch naturalist and merchant **Anthony van Leeuwenhoeck** (1632-1723) perfected the instrument, building a **single** optical microscope (so-called because it had one lens) bringing **the enlargement up to 300 times**. Without possessing any scientific qualification, he discovered, by observing through the microscope, the **red blood corpuscles**, **spermatozoa** and **protozoa**, single-celled organisms, such as the amoeba.

Working spectacles from the beginning of the 1900s

below right, the cutter for oval lenses
bottom picture, case for lenses dating from the 1920s

Did you know...

The lenses used by Hans and Zacharias Jansen were invented at least 300 years before. Even in the times of the ancient Romans and the Middle Ages, people used lenses for commercial and ocular (eyesight) purposes. But before the Jansens, nobody had the idea of combining the two together. The invention of the microscope is also linked to the name of Italian Francesco Fontana who made a similar instrument at the same time as the two Dutch inventors.

THE THIRD EYE

It is thanks to the microscope that people have discovered so much about many natural processes which had been a mystery for so long. One example is the **circulation of blood**. English doctor **William Harvey** was the first to maintain that the heart is an organ which pumps blood around the body – but his belief was not accepted by the scientific world until many years afterwards. It was another doctor, Italian **Marcello Malpighi**, who confirmed Harvey's theory in **1661**, by observing **through the microscope the movement of blood through the capillaries**.

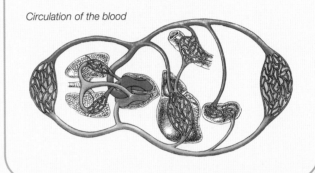

Circulation of the blood

William Harvey

Galileo's microscope – he called this his perspicillum and then 'eye-piece'

Modern microscope

HOMUNCULI, OR LITTLE MEN

Anthony van Leeuwenhoeck discovered **spermatozoa** through the microscope on 9 October 1679. Van Leeuwenhoeck, thinking that these were microscopic creatures, described them as *homunculi*, meaning 'little men'. His discovery was conveyed by letter to the **Royal Society, London**, but this was ignored until 1875, when the German scientist Oskar Hertwig described the structure and the function of the human **ovules** and **spermatozoa**, explaining how **human fertilization** takes place.

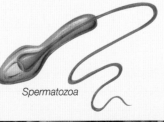

Spermatozoa

When did Hertz discover electromagnetic waves?

In November **1886**, 20-year old **Rudolf Heinrich Hertz** demonstrated the **existence** of **electromagnetic waves**. The young German physicist was using an **electric oscillator** when he succeeded in obtaining rapid electrical oscillations and transmitted these between two circuits at a distance of 1.5 metres. Proceeding with his experiments, Hertz discovered the **principle of tuning** which consisted of putting two circuits in resonance – that is, both at the same frequency of sound waves. The tuning principle would be used later in the development of radio.

The life of Hertz was amazingly creative, especially taking into account that he died at only 37 years of age. He was dedicated to research and to teaching at the Universities of Berlin, Kiel, Karlsruhe and Bonn. The Royal Society of London elected him as a member.

Rudolf Heinrich Hertz

Oscillator circuit used by Guglielmo Marconi for his studies on radio

Did you know...

Hertz was a very cultured man, who could **read and write in many languages**, including **Italian** and **ancient Greek**. The famous physicist Hermann von Helmholtz had been Hertz's professor at Berlin University. When he learned of the death of Hertz, Helmholtz wrote in the preface of the work of his pupil, *Principles of Mechanics*, 'In classical ancient times, it would have been said that he was sacrificed because of the envy of the gods'.

THANKS TO HERTZ!

The unit of measurement to establish the frequency of a sound wave is calculated in **hertz (Hz)**. The normal human ear is able to perceive sounds of between 16,000 and 20,000 Hz.

When was the atom discovered?

In **1803** in England, chemist **John Dalton** demonstrated the existence of atoms and gave them a scientific definition for the first time. According to this definition, each element is characterized by a particular type of basic particle, called an atom, which determines the property of an element.

The atom, therefore, can be defined as the smallest part of matter with chemical-physical properties which remain unchanged.

For instance – the element **water (H_2O)** is made up of hydrogen and oxygen, and its composition (two atoms of hydrogen for each atom of oxygen) is a sort of **identity code** which remains unaltered under all conditions.

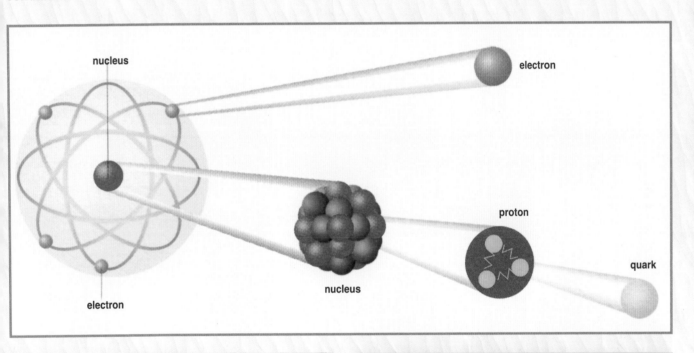

WHO WERE THE FIRST TO TALK OF ATOMS?

The Greek philosopher **Democrito** (circa 460-370 BC) was the first to formulate the **existence of an elementary unit** and indivisible matter which he called 'the **atom**' (a Greek word meaning 'indivisible'). His speculation on the existence of atoms remained purely theoretical, because it could not be demonstrated scientifically.

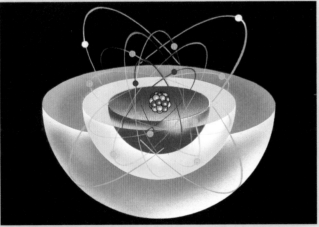

When was the Internet born?

The Internet began in the **1970s** in the USA during the period of the so-called '**cold war**', when the two great powers of the Soviet Union and the USA were competing for world supremacy, but without going to war. In 1969 some American universities invented **Arpanet** (a forerunner of the Internet) for the Department of Defense, who feared a breakdown of communication in the event of a Soviet attack. Arpanet was a network which enabled **communication and an exchange of data through computers** (at that time, **only four**!) and which could guarantee the transmission of information, even during confict.

The worldwide network **Internet has existed since 1992**. A group of researchers led by English physicist **Tim Berners-Lee** based at the information laboratory of **CERN (European Centre for Nuclear Research)** in Geneva, Switzerland, invented the **World Wide Web** – a system of access to information which enables millions of computer users throughout the world to communicate with each other.

Internet enables millions of computer users all over the world to communicate with each other

Did you know...

The @ symbol has many nicknames. In Italy it is called the 'snail' *chiocciola*; in Denmark, 'elephant's trunk', *snabel-a*; in Holland, 'monkey's tail', *apestaart;* in Germany, 'monkey-spider', *klammeraffe* and in Norway 'spiral cinnamon cake', *kanec-bolle*.

YOU'VE GOT MAIL...
For speed and reliability, electronic mail (email) has overtaken ordinary mail. In 2002 it was estimated that throughout the world 31 billion emails were sent each day, more than 11 thousand billion per year.

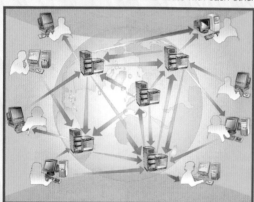

WHERE DOES THE @ SIGN FOR THE INTERNET COME FROM?

The origin of this sign is very old. Contrary to what most people may think, it comes from an ancient Egyptian or Mesopotamian hieroglyph which was used as a sign of measurement. Also, the ancient Romans, from about the sixth to the seventh century AD used the @ sign as an abbreviation for the word 'ad' (meaning 'to' or 'at') when writing by dictation. The symbol @ means 'at' in the English language.

Who invented the first clock?

Mechanical clock

Water clock

From the dawn of humankind, people have been conscious of their need to measure time, so that they could regulate all that they had to do. At first, people told the time by watching the **movements of the moon**, as it made one complete turn on its axis every 28 days. In about 3000 BC, **priests** and **Assyrian-Babylonian astronomers** divided **the day into 24 hours** of equal duration, then subdivided **each hour into 60 minutes**. It seems that the first instrument used by people to measure time was a solar clock, a type of sundial, invented in **Egypt in 2000 BC**. This consisted of a pole which was illuminated by the Sun and projected its shadow on to a quarter-circle space on which was drawn the hours. Some centuries later there came the first real **sundial**, with a straight pole called a **gnomon** which projected its shadow on to a horizontal space. By observing the position of the shadow as it moved from east to west, following the curved path of the Sun, it was possible to establish the hour.

At the same time in Egypt a **water clock** was invented. The oldest one found so far dates from about 1360 BC. This was a stone vase with a hole in the bottom, through which the water flowed out. On the inside of the vase notches were made at regular intervals to indicate the passing of the hours, based on the quantity of water remaining in the vase. The first mechanical clocks were made in **Europe** from about the **thirteenth century**.

Solar clock

These told the time by sounding a bell at certain times of the day, but at first there was no clock face or hands. In 1364 Italian **Giovanni Dondi** became the first to put a face on a mechanical clock. His clock had seven faces which, as well as showing the hour, also showed the movements of the planets which were known at the time.

WHERE IS THE OLDEST CLOCK?

The oldest working clock in the world is in Strasbourg cathedral. Work on the clock began in 1547. It was built to replace an earlier clock which was made in the fourteenth century. The huge face is divided into three parts to show the day, the months and the phases of the moon combined with the movement of the stars. At mid-day, a line of figures emerge, representing the apostles in procession, and a cockerel which opens its wings and sings. As well as all this, the clock has the figure of a wizard who holds a water clock, which he tips up at each hour.

Astronomical clock at Strasbourg

How do clouds form?

The heat of the Sun makes the **waters of the seas and rivers evaporate**. This evaporation produces **water vapour**, which **rises up**. When this water vapour comes into **contact with cold air**, it condenses – that means, it is transformed into **tiny drops of water** which then gather together to form clouds.

The tops of mountains are often shrouded by clouds which form when warm air comes into contact with the cold mountain. Then, as the warm air rises up the mountain slopes, it is cooled by the low temperature, and finally condenses into droplets of water and then cloud.

Different types of cloud can be distinguished by their shape and the distance from the surface of the Earth. Clouds can be divided into four main groups – **cirrus, cumulus, stratus and nimbus**.

SUMMER CLOUDS IN THE CITY

During the summer, there are often violent downpours of rain. These are not always due to local weather conditions, but physical phenomenon.

The **asphalt** and **cement** which covers so much of city areas both **attract and hold a lot of heat**. As a reaction, the asphalt and cement covering tries to lose this heat as fast as it can, and so the heat evaporates into water vapour which rises up and condenses into drops of water which comprise clouds.

When these drops become large and heavy, they fall to the ground in the form of rain. But before hitting the ground, one droplet of water increases in size by about one million times.

10.000 metres

cirrus

cirrocumulus

cirrostratus

altocumulus

altostratus

66

Where do tsunami come from?

Tsunami is a Japanese word which means **wave** (nami) and **port** (tsu). A tsunami happens following an earthquake, a volcanic eruption, explosions, landslides and movements of the Earth's tectonic plates in the depths of the sea. Seismic waves increase in the water, making enormous waves rise up which move at great speed. Near to coasts, **these waves can reach the breadth and height of a wall up to 40 metres high**. A tsunami is like a 'sea steam-roller' which destroys everything in its path, especially in coastal regions. The danger of the tsunami is that its force **cannot be detected** until it is almost at its height, because it begins under the sea, where nobody can see what is happening.

WHERE IS THE CENTRE OF THE TSUNAMI TO BE FOUND?

The **city of Hilo** on the north-east coast of the **island of Hawaii** has often had devastating tsunami waves, because of its particularly exposed location. Since 1948, the **Pacific Tsunami Warning System** has been in operation in this zone of the Pacific. Its purpose is to monitor and prevent as far as possible the arrival of these terrible waves.

Also, the Japanese coast has often been hit by the violence of the tsunami. In 1700, a tsunami devastated the coast of Hondo region of the islands of Japan.

The famous wood-block colour print The Great Wave by Japanese artist Hokusai

Who discovered x-rays?

On the cold evening of 22 December 1895, German physicist **Wilhelm Conrad Röntgen** took the first-ever X-ray photograph, which was of **his wife's hand, complete with her wedding ring**. Röntgen had arrived at his discovery by pure chance. Whilst carrying out some experiments using a cathode-ray tube, he noticed that this tube emitted particular rays, which he called '**X-rays**' because their origin was unknown. Röntgen found that the invisible X-rays went through soft tissue, such as the skin, but were blocked when they met dense tissue, such as bone. He understood the importance of his discovery and its possible medical applications, and so it was that the science of **radiology** came about. Röntgen was awarded the Nobel Prize for physics in 1901 for his important discovery.

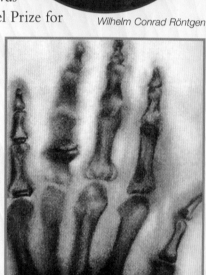

Wilhelm Conrad Röntgen

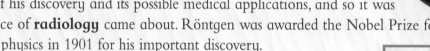

X-ray image of the hand of Röntgen's wife, showing her wedding ring

The first radiography machine

Did you know...

The first to use the **X** sign to indicate something unknown was **René Descartes**, 16th century philosopher and mathematician. He introduced the letter **X** into algebra to express an unknown quantity.

Who was Nobel?

Alfred Bernhard Nobel

Alfred Bernhard Nobel was a Swedish chemist and industrialist. He founded an industrial empire, thanks to his discovery of the explosive **dynamite**. On his death on 10 December 1896, he left a considerable part of his fortune to a foundation with the purpose of presenting a prize each year to those people whose work in science or literature had contributed to the progress of humanity and maintenance of peace.

The **first award of the Nobel Prize was on 10 December 1901, at the Royal Academy of Music, Stockholm.** There are six categories for which the Nobel Prize can be awarded – physics, chemistry, medicine, literature, economics and peace.

The Nobel Prize award ceremony takes place each year on 10 December, the anniversary of Nobel's death.

Apart from the honour of receiving the award, prize-winners also receive a considerable sum of money – about 1,000,000 Euro. This money is given to enable prize-winners to progress with their studies and research without having to worry about earning money.

WHAT IS THE IG® NOBEL PRIZE?

The Ig® Nobel Prize is awarded for studies defined by the founders as those which 'first make people laugh, then make them think'.

From 1991, each year at Harvard University in the USA the **Ig® Nobel Prizes** (the word 'ignoble' meaning 'unworthy' or 'worthless) have been awarded.

Categories are not so rigid as those for the Nobel Prize, and application must be shown towards serious scientific study.

For instance – in 1992, the Ig® Nobel Prize for physics was awarded to Ramesh Balasubramaniam and Michael Turvey for **explaining the dynamics of hula-hooping**.

The prize for chemistry was for research into **using advanced technology to convert liquid from the River Thames into a transparent form of water, which for precautionary reasons has been made unavailable to consumers**.

Did you know...

In the history of the Nobel Prize so far, four people have won the prize two or more times. In **1903** Polish-born scientist **Marie Curie**, together with her husband **Pierre** were awarded **the Nobel prize for physics**, after discovering two radio-active elements – Radium and Polonium. **Eight years later**, they were awarded the same prize, **but for chemistry**. The USA chemist **Linus Carl Pauling** was awarded **the 1954 chemistry and the Nobel Prize for peace in 1962**, in recognition of his stand against nuclear experiments. The USA physicist **John Bardeen** received the **Nobel Prize for Physics in 1956** and again in 1972. English biochemist **Frederick Ranger** won the Nobel Prize for chemistry in **1958** and again in **1980**.

How does a thermometer work?

The normal body temperature for a human being is about 37°C, and is regulated by certain centres of the brain

When any liquid is heated up, the liquid molecules expand. A thermometer makes use of this phenomenon by increasing the temperature of liquid mercury to establish the temperature of an external body.

A thermometer consists of a round bulb of glass containing the liquid mercury, which is the colour of silver, and a thin, tapered tube. When the temperature of a human body is measured, the mercury in the glass bulb absorbs the heat of the body and dilates, expanding up along the tapered tube. The notched signs along the tube denote the temperature of the body, simply by reading the number corresponding to the level reached by the mercury in the bulb.

To take a temperature again, it is necessary to shake the thermometer to make the liquid mercury descend to the bottom of the tube.

The first **medical thermometer** was made in 1616 by the Italian doctor **Santorio Santorio**.

WHY DOES WATER AT 24° SEEM COLDER THAN AIR AT THE SAME TEMPERATURE?

If a human body comes into contact with a material which has a temperature which is lower, then some of the body heat flows towards it – for example, if a hand clutches a cold steel rod, then the rod will get warm.

The process of **transmission of heat** is quicker if the material is a **good conductor of heat**.

Air is a poor conductor of heat, whereas water can conduct heat 26 times faster than air. For this reason, to dive into a swimming pool with a temperature of 24° causes a sensation which is far colder than entering a room of the same temperature.

Did you know...

The first to invent **air conditioning** was the American **Willis H. Carrier**. In 1902 he took out a patent for a machine which could draw in air and cool it by making it pass through a circuit cooled by water, and then feeding the cooled air back into the surroundings.

What makes an echo?

An echo consists of a **repetition of a sound** caused by the reflection ('bouncing back') of a sound wave against an obstacle.

When an echo happens, the distance between the sound and the obstacle must be at least 20 metres. This phenomenon frequently happens in mountain regions. Here, sound waves can easily hit obstacles, such as the sides of a mountain, and be reflected back.

The instruments which use the phenomenon of the echo are the **megaphone** and the **sonar** which uses the echo to measure the distance of objects in water.

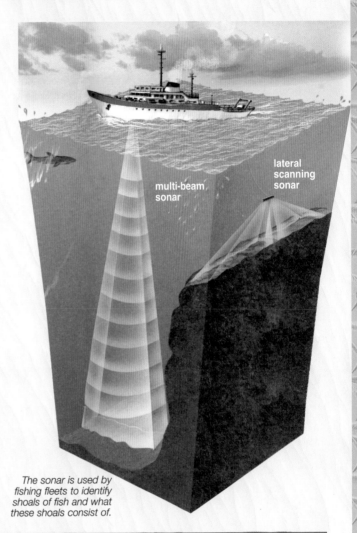

multi-beam sonar

lateral scanning sonar

The sonar is used by fishing fleets to identify shoals of fish and what these shoals consist of.

HOW DOES AN ELECTRIC FAN PRODUCE COOLNESS?

The human body has a temperature of 36 – 37°C. The temperature of our surroundings is often lower. So, to balance this difference in temperature, the body must give out heat into the external air, by a process called **convection**: the warm air from the body mixes with the cooler air to disperse heat.

When we use an electric fan, this causes a greater exchange of cold air near the skin and so the body gives out a larger quantity of heat. This dispersal makes the body sense a pleasant **feeling of coolness**.

When was DNA discovered?

The 'double-helix' structure of DNA

On 15 April 1953 in the journal *Nature* there appeared an article, *Molecular Structure of nucleid acid: a structure for Desoxyribose Nucleid Acid*.

This article was to change the face of science in general. Molecular biologists **James Dewey Watson** and **Francis Harry Crick** had discovered the double-helix structure of **DNA** (**Desoxyribose Nucleic Acid**) and its function. DNA is found in all chromosomes in cells and carries genetic information, which is why it is also referred to as the 'genetic code'.

The molecules of DNA are made up of two long chains of organic compounds called **nucleotides** – **adenine**, **cytosine**, **guanine** and **thymine** – woven into a spiral which creates a structure defined as a '**double helix**'. All the information on the life of a human being is 'written' in DNA and all physical characteristics (height, colour of hair, body structure, etc.) are determined by the structure of DNA molecules. For their sensational discovery, Watson and Crick and another biologist, **Maurice Hugh Frederick Wilkins, were awarded the 1962 Nobel Prize for physiology and medicine**.

DNA IS THE BEST EVIDENCE

When a crime is complex and the guilty person is not yet charged, the Police can get proof through **DNA**. This is done by carrying out a **test, extracting a sample of DNA from blood, hair, nails or other body substances** found at the scene of the crime and then comparing this sample against a sample of DNA obtained from the suspect. If the two samples match, then the suspect is guilty – because each individual has a 'genetic code' which is unique to that person and nobody else. Copies of each molecule in the DNA sample are made for any further investigation through the chemical process **PRC (polymerase chain reaction)**.

Who invented the battery?

The **battery** was invented by the Italian physicist **Alessandro Volta** in **1799**. The first description of the invention appeared in a letter of 20 March 1800 addressed to J. Banks, President of the Royal Society, London. Fascinated by the study of electrical phenomena, which came to the fore in the late 1700s, Alessandro Volta was inspired by another Italian, anatomist, **Luigi Galvani**.

In 1791, Galvani had discovered that if the muscles of a dead frog were touched by two different metals, zinc and copper, the frogs' legs twitched and contracted.

Galvani came to the conclusion that this contraction was caused by electricity in the animal tissue. His theory was presented to the Academy of Science in Bologna in a paper entitled *De viribus electricitatis in motu muscolari animalium* ('On proving electricity in the muscle movement of animals'). But when Volta repeated Galvani's experiments, he saw that the electricity did not come from the frog, but flowed from the contact between the two metals. This observation led to a dispute between the two scientists, which led to controversy between the University of Padua, where Volta taught, and the University of Bologna, where Galvani worked.

But this controversy inspired Volta to continue with his experiments. He discovered that when two different metals connected by a wire were immersed in a saline substance called the electrolyte, the wire attracted an electrical charge. Volta built his first battery by a series of discs of zinc and copper piled up alternately and each disc separated by a circle of fabric which had been soaked in a saline substance, all connected by a conductor wire. The chemical reaction between the two metals and the saline substance produced a flow of electrons from one disc to another, producing electric current.

Galvani carries out experiments on electricity in animals

A FAMOUS ADMIRER

After having presented his invention at the Royal Society, London, **Alessandro Volta** was **invited to Paris on 7 November 1801** by a very famous admirer, **Napoleon Bonaparte**. The Emperor of France, after getting to know about Volta's discovery, invited him to his court, so that he could present a demonstration of his battery. As payment, Bonaparte conferred on Volta the **Legion d'Onore**, the title 'King of Electricity' and a prize of 6000 lire.

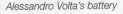
Alessandro Volta's battery

How do traffic signals work?

Traffic signals work by a 'timer' which is controlled by a computer and which illuminates **red**, **amber** and **green** lights at regular intervals.

In recent years, the number of road vehicles have increased so much that it has been necessary to have an 'intelligent' installation – one which can regulate the traffic signals, automatically changing the lights from red to green according to the flow of traffic.

An automatic traffic signal is controlled by sensors or tele-cameras which can reveal immediately the density of cruising traffic. This information is then relayed to the central traffic control, which regulates the traffic signals.

The **first traffic signals** in history comprised a **gas-operated system** installed in London in **1868**.

In **1914** the first **electric system** with three-colour traffic lights was installed in New York.

The signals – **red (stop), amber (caution or wait) and green (go)** – were operated manually by an employee.

The **automatic traffic signals which we know** were only introduced in **1926**.

Did you know...

Traffic has been a problem since the days of the ancient Romans. In many European cities, **chariots were banned during daylight hours**, following the example of **Julius Caesar** in the **1st century AD**. Pedestrian crossings on main roads are controlled differently throughout the world. Some countries use a red light with the words WAIT or STOP, followed by a green light, with the message GO, or CROSS WITH CARE. Others use a combination of traffic lights and flashing signs reading 'STOP' then 'WALK, DON'T RUN'.

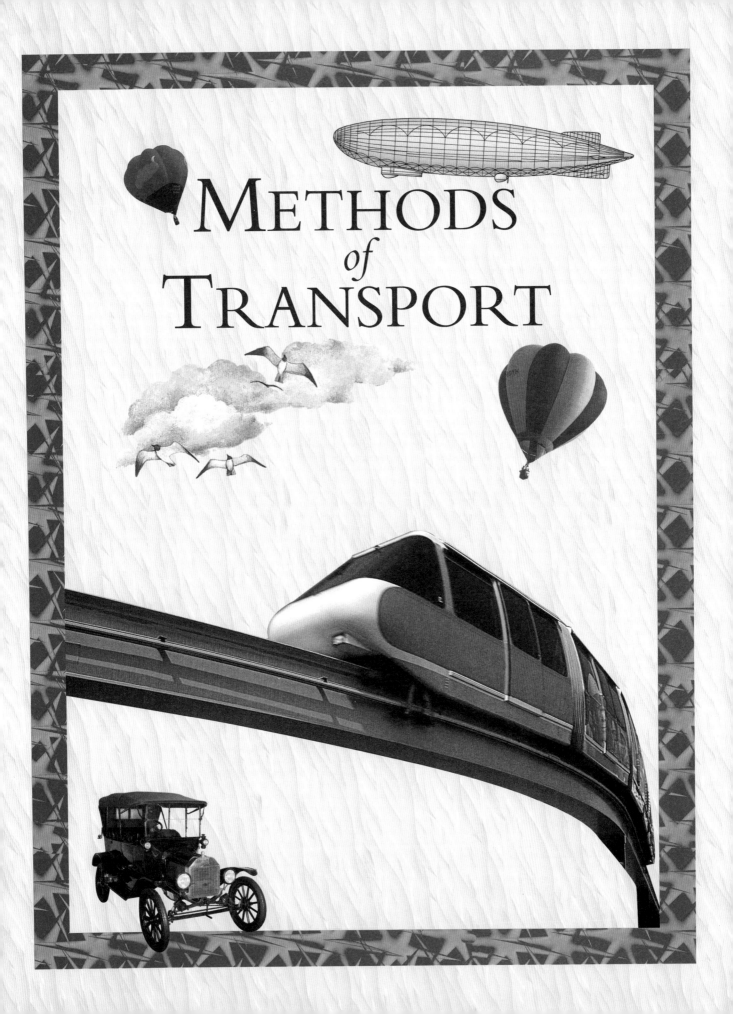

Methods
of
Transport

Who drove the first car?

The French military engineer **Joseph Cugnot** is widely accepted as the first motorist in history. In 1770, he designed and built the first motorized vehicle. It was actually a sort of tricycle with a two-cylinder steam engine which could go at about 5 kilometres per hour. To come nearer to the cars which we use today, we need to move forward a few years: at the 1867 Paris Exposition, German engineer **Nikolaus Otto** presented his invention, without which the car could not have been developed. This invention was the **petrol-driven combustion engine**, which Otto had built in partnership with **Eugen Langen**. In 1883, two other Germans, **Gottlieb Daimler** and **Wilhelm Maybach**, built an **internal-combustion engine** which was lighter than Otto and Langen's, and in 1885, **Carl Frederich Benz** built the first **three-wheeled car** incorporating Daimler's engine. This vehicle reached a speed of 15 kilometres per hour and was the first car to take to the road. In 1889, Daimler installed the **petrol-driven engine** not in a tricycle, but an **elegant four-wheeled carriage**. Four years later, Benz built his first four-wheeled car - a luxury very few people could afford, because it was so expensive.

Model T Ford

conveyor belt car manufacture

Did you know...

During his first test drive on the road, **Joseph Cugnot drove into a wall** - making this the first car accident in history!
Today, his first vehicle is kept in the National Museum of Transport in Paris.

Daimler's two-cylinder engine

CONVEYOR BELT

*In 1896, American **Henry Ford** built a four-wheeled motorized vehicle - and in 1908, Ford revolutionized the world of transport with his Model T Ford car. Henry Ford radically changed car manufacture by introducing the **conveyor belt** system. This consists of producing vehicles in series - that is, by assembling together all the parts of the car which had already been produced separately. Only 350 parts were needed to assemble the Model T Ford, and this made the car easy to build and to repair. A Model T Ford could be built in just **one hour and a half** - until that time, it had taken at least thirteen hours work to build a car. With his conveyor belt system, Ford could save working time, cut costs and so sell the Model T Ford at a price which was much lower, compared to other cars on the market. It was a great success - over **15 million Model T Ford cars** were sold!*

The inventor Carl Benz, centre, and his family in a vehicle he constructed, from a photograph of 1895

When did the first airship take to the sky?

On 24 September 1852 in Versailles near Paris, the first **airship**, the **Giffard I** rose up into the air. It was 44 metres long and had a non-rigid, tapered structure.

It had been built by **Henri-Jacques Giffard**, an ex railway worker who was passionate about flight. Giffard flew his giant airship for over 31 kilometres and surveyed Paris at a speed of 10 kilometres per hour. The age of airships had begun!

The difference between an airship and a hot-air balloon is mainly the tapered shape of the airship. Inside, the **Giffard I** was filled with hydrogen, a gas which is lighter than air. It was powered by a steam engine which turned a propeller and was steered by a rudder.

In 1894, the steam engine was substituted by a combustion engine, designed by **Albert Santos-Dumont**. At the beginning of the 1900s, due to the work and the interest of **German Count Zeppelin**, airships quickly became famous and they soon became a popular means of transport.

The Giffard I

Italian airships, P.2 and P.3

Airships were used for the transport of goods and also for military purposes – during the First World War, London was bombed by German airships.

Zeppelin's first airship had a rigid aluminium structure covered in cotton and treated with a varnish to make it weather resistant. It had a cabin to carry passengers and the crew and was 126 metres long.

On 2 July 1900, the **Zeppelin I, flight number LZ1** flew over Lake Constance, reaching a height of 400 metres and covering 6 kilometres in 17 minutes, with five people on board.

In the 1920s, transport by airship had become the way for the rich and famous to cross the Atlantic in luxury, which was why a Zeppelin airship was called 'the flying hotel'. However, due to the hydrogen catching fire, travel by airship came to an end in the 1930s.

The Graf Zeppelin airship

Cut-out section plan of an airship

AROUND THE WORLD IN...

*In 1929, **the airship Graf Zeppelin, flight number LZ127 went around the world in 12 days**, landing only in Tokyo, Los Angeles and Lakehurst, in New Jersey. Within nine years, this airship had crossed the Atlantic **139 times**!*

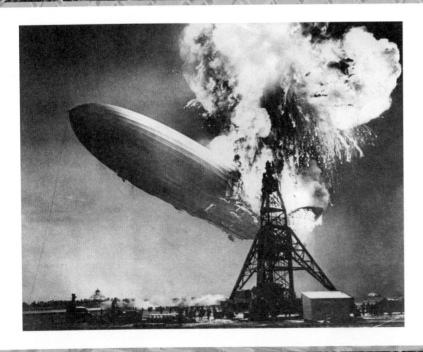

THE HINDENBURG, GIANT OF THE SKIES

The Hindenburg, flight number LZ129 was the largest airship ever built. It was 245 metres long and was constructed in 1936 in Count Zeppelin's German workshops.

On 6 May 1937, after carrying out 63 trans-Atlantic flights, the Hindenburg caught fire whilst landing (photograph, left). 35 people died in the flames and 62 were injured. After that, no passenger-carrying airships went into service.

How is a ship built?

The building of a **ship** begins with the construction of the **hull** – the basic structure which enables the ship to float. This is done in various stages. It begins with a **plan** which is produced in the **drawing offices** of the ship-builders. At this stage, marine engineers study all the strains which the ship will be under when it takes to the sea.

Complex calculations are necessary, in order to decide on the size of the various parts of the vessel, as well as a detailed analysis of each part of the ship. The structure of the **ship's engines** is also studied at the same time.

All this leads to the actual construction of the ship. First comes the **supply** of the necessary materials, and the **working arrangement** of all the parts. Then comes the **building of the keel** and the sides. When this is done, the whole hull is sometimes '**launched**' (pushed into the water). Otherwise, the hull is constructed in a dry dock. To make sure the ship is seaworthy, there are trials at each stage of construction and these take into account the structure of the ship and the performance of the engines.

Finally, there is the **installation** on board of all the necessary equipment (radio, radar, computers, etc.) followed by all the furnishings and fittings.

Construction of a ship's hull

The launch of a ship

WHAT IS THE LARGEST PASSENGER LINER IN THE WORLD?

Its name is **Queen Mary 2** and it is the largest passenger ship ever built!

It is 345 metres long (about three and a half times the length of a football pitch) and 45 metres more than the height of the Eiffel Tower. It is 41 metres wide and 72 metres high, with 17 bridges. Its weight is 150,000 tonnes and its engines work at a rate of 157,000 horse-power - able to produce enough energy for a city of 250,000 people. Its maximum speed is 30 knots, with a cruising speed of 28.5 knots.

The liner has a crew of 1253 people and it can carry 1367 passengers, each spending up to 30,000 Euro for an eight-day cruise. The time taken to build Queen Mary 2 is a world record – 8,000,000 hours!

Queen Mary 2

naval shipyard in Kure, Japan

Who flew the first aeroplane?

Bicycle manufacturers, brothers **Orville and Wilbur Wright**, took to the skies on 17 December 1903 in their flying machine, a biplane with two propellers and a light, petrol-powered engine of only 8 horse-power called **Flyer**. On the beach at **Kitty Hawk**, in North Carolina, Orville flew for 12 seconds, covering a distance of 36 metres at a height of three metres.

The only witness to this event was his brother, Wilbur, and some local fishermen who did not realize what they were seeing.

But it was only in 1908 that true success came to the Wright brothers, when they obtained wider recognition after demonstration flights in France and in the USA. By that time, their flying machine, now much improved, had already travelled more than 100 kilometres!

The Wright brothers' Flyer

Did you know...

The first aircraft to fly appeared in the 16th century – it was a **paper aeroplane**!

THE FIRST NEW YORK TO PARIS FLIGHT

American aviator **Charles Augustus Lindbergh** in May 1927 completed the first solo trans-Atlantic flight on board his monoplane *The Spirit of Saint Louis*.

Lindbergh flew for 33 and a half hours non-stop, covering over 5800 kilometres. Lindbergh recounted his extraordinary story in his book *Spirit of Saint Louis*.

WHAT IS THE ORIGIN OF THE MAY-DAY SIGNAL?

During the First World War, as British pilots surveyed France in order to bomb the German lines, they had to do battle with the squadrons led by German aviator Manfred von Richthofen, nicknamed the **Red Baron**. When their aircraft were hit, the British pilots called for help via their radios, using the French words 'M'aidez!' (meaning, 'help me'). In 1948, the distress signal 'May Day' was officially recognized at international level - and today, all countries when they hear '**May Day**' know that it is a request for help from the captain of a ship or the pilot of an aircraft.

Manfred von Richthofen, the Red Baron

WHAT IS THE 'BLACK BOX'?

The '**black box**' (which is actually red in colour) is an important record of flight which is installed in all military and civil aircraft. It makes a record of all that happens on board. An aircraft has two black boxes - one for messages to and from the Control Tower, and the other for information on the flight. This information is kept in 25 x 12 x 12 centimetre containers of stainless steel, with walls 6 - 7 millimetres thick and wrapped in a special foam to protect it from heat in the event of fire or explosion. A black box is placed near the tail of an aircraft, because this is usually the section which is least damaged when an aircraft crashes.

Who were the Montgolfier brothers?

Joseph-Michel and **Jacques Étienne Montgolfier** were the sons of a French paper manufacturer. After having taken over the running of their father's business, they concentrated on experimenting with their inventions. Both were fascinated by flight and they designed and built the first **hot-air balloon**. Their first experiment was carried out inside the large workrooms of their paper-making factory. But on 4 June 1783, they launched their first unmanned hot-air balloon into the sky at Annonay, near Lyon. This flew for 17 minutes, covering a distance of 2 kilometres. On 19 September 1783, after having made a few final modifications, the Montgolfier brothers put on board the first passengers to fly - a **sheep**, a **cockerel** and a **goose**. The three animals survived their eight-minute flight unharmed (the cockerel's wings had been clipped, but this was only for convenience, so that it could not fly off) and this led to the first flight by human beings. The spectacle was attended by **King Louis XVI** and his wife, **Queen Marie-Antoinette**. On 21 November 1783, in the grounds of the Castle Muette in the Bois de Boulogne, a large park on the outskirts of Paris, the **first hot-air balloon piloted by human beings**, physicist **Jean François Pilâtre de Rozier** and the **Marchese d'Arlandes**, rose up in flight. The hot-air balloon reached a height of 1000 metres and flew for 25 minutes, covering eight kilometres on board a hot-air balloon 20.7 metres high and with a diameter of 13.6 metres. In recognition of their invention, the Montgolfier brothers were made members of the French Académie des Sciences and knighted by King Louis XVI.

Did you know...

The two Montgolfier brothers were also interested in other inventions. Joseph built a parachute, plus an instrument for extracting the juice from fruit and a hydraulic press. Jacques is also famous for the invention of tissue paper.

Below and below left: Two prints showing the first attempts at flight

HOW DID THE HOT-AIR BALLOON RISE INTO THE AIR?

The Montgolfiers followed a simple rule of science - hot air rises. And so they knew that when a light covering was filled with hot air, this covering would also rise into the air. First, the Montgolfiers filled the balloon with cold air, which they heated up by burning a fire in a steel brazier fixed underneath the balloon.

JOYS AND SORROWS

One of the two people who first succeeded in flying was also one of the first to perish in an air accident.
*On 15 July 1785, Jean François Pilâtre de Rozier was killed **whilst trying to cross the English Channel** on board a hot-air balloon . This had two balloons - one filled with air, the other with hydrogen. After only fifteen minutes flight, the hydrogen-filled balloon caught fire and exploded, killing **Pilâtre de Rozier** and his flying companion, **Pierre-Ange Romain**, the man who also built the ill-fated balloon.*

The hot-air balloon used by Pilâtre de Rozier

AROUND THE WORLD

In March 1999 the hot-air balloon **Breiting Orbiter III** took 19 days to fly around the world, covering 42,800 kilometres without ever landing!

ONE EYE ON WEIGHT...

Lady Letitia Sage was an English noble-woman who was very keen to fly. Her dream came true, flying with two other passengers in a hot-air balloon - but, unfortunately, one of her fellow passengers had to make the balloon descend very hurriedly before it crashed down. The reason? The lady **weighed over 100 kilos**!

When was the first submersible built?

The TurtleS

A submersible can be defined as a vehicle which can go underwater. In 1775, American **David Bushnell** built the first submersible which he called **Turtle** because it was shaped like a turtle shell. It made its first dive on 7 June 1776 in New York harbour, where the Statue of Liberty now stands. **Turtle** was **moved by two propellers**, **hand-controlled** by one man, and it was later used by the American fleet in 1776 during the first War of Independence against the British battleship, Eagle. In 1800, American inventor Robert Fulton built the **Nautilus**. This submersible was cylinder-shaped with a wooden hull covered with copper, 6 metres long and 1.8 wide and could carry eight men. It could remain underwater for eight hours. The Nautilus was equipped with a **compass**, a **barometer** and a **turret**.

By the end of the 18th century, submersibles were **diesel-powered** and then **electric**, instead of being manually-operated. During the First and Second World Wars, underwater vehicles became the 'hidden army' of each nation, with battles being fought beneath the sea waves. During the years 1940-1945 submersibles gave way to **submarines** which could remain underwater, largely due to the invention of the **snorkel**, a tube through which supplies of fresh air could be obtained, without the submarine having to surface and reveal itself to the enemy. Following continuing progress and constant testing with new sources of energy, in 1955, the USA built the **first nuclear-powered submarine**. This was also called **Nautilus** and it was powered by a nuclear reactor, designed to stay underwater for thousands of kilometres. It was the first submarine to sail under the ice of the **North Pole**.

The Nautilus

Submarines ready to dive

HOW DOES A SUBMARINE WORK?

As soon as the Commander orders the submarine to dive, water is let into special **ballast tanks**. This makes the submarine heavy, whilst the **fins** are positioned in such a way as to produce a downward thrust. When the submarine reaches the required depth, the fins are then re-positioned for the submarine to maintain a horizontal position.

To rise up again, water is pumped out of the ballast tanks, and the fins are again re-positioned to enable the submarine to rise to the surface. The first part to emerge is the **turret**, with the **periscope**, then the **radio antenna** and the **radio**. On the surface, a submarine uses **diesel motors**, whilst underwater it runs on **electric engines** which are charged by a huge battery.

Photographs above and below left - submarines in port
Below, cut-out section plans of a submarine

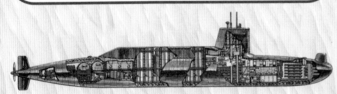

HOW MANY COUNTRIES HAVE NUCLEAR-POWERED SUBMARINES?

The USA, Russia, France, the UK and China all have nuclear submarines, but we can also add India and Chile to the list.

At full speed, the fastest nuclear submarines can reach **80 kilometres per hour**, **descending to a depth of up to 650 metres** and they can remain underwater for as long as is required; the necessary oxygen is produced by special equipment.

The largest submarine in the world is the Severstahl, code-name TK-20. This Russian submarine is 173 metres long and has 100,000 horse-power.

Who invented the monorail?

The Sydney monorail, Australia

The first **monorail** was opened in **1887** and linked Ballybunion and Listowel in Co. Kerry, Ireland. As indicated by the name 'monorail', this had just one iron track on which wagons and carriages ran on either side, suspended just above the ground and of equal size to maintain balance.

In 1911, the American **William Boyes** invented the elevated monorail which ran high above ground level. The monorail is a method of transport which is constantly expanding, especially in countries such as China, Japan, Korea and Singapore, where there are serious traffic problems due to over-population.

The city of **Sydney** in Australia has a reliable and comfortable monorail used every year by four million people.

WHEN WAS THE FIRST UNDERGROUND BUILT?

The **first underground** system was opened on 10 January 1863 in **London**, a city in which, even at that time, had serious traffic problems. The carriages were pulled by a steam locomotive, powered by coal. This produced a lot of smoke, and so there had to be openings in the underground tunnels. The length of the line was 6 kilometres and it ran **between Bishop's Road, Paddington and Farringdon Street stations**. For the first time, passengers could also admire the inside of the carriages which were illuminated by gas lighting.

UNDERGROUND

WHERE IS THE LONGEST UNDERGROUND?

The London Underground is 388 kilometres long and has 12 lines which link up all areas of Greater London. Londoners and regular users call London Underground 'the tube'.

When was the first railway line built?

In 1825, the **Stockton to Darlington** Railway opened in England. It was 34 kilometres long and open trucks were pulled by a coal-powered, steam locomotive built by the English engineer, **George Stephenson**, who also drove the first train. The locomotive was called **Locomotion** and the first carriage **Experiment**.

A few years later, George Stephenson astounded the world by building a super-speed model of locomotive - at least, for that time. He called this **The Rocket** and it flew like a rocket at a speed of 50 kilometres an hour along the Liverpool to Manchester line which opened in 1830.

The Rocket locomotive

TRAINS TRAVEL ON THE LEFT...

*It is probably because the first railway opened in England, where all traffic travels on the left, that all railways now **travel on the left**. When other European countries bought carriages, locomotives and wagons from the English, they also adopted the method of railways travelling on the left - because the first steam locomotives were driven on the left side to avoid getting in the way of the fireman who would be shovelling coal into the fire-box to heat the water in the locomotive boiler to produce the steam power which it needed.*

The highest railway in the world, in the Andes

WHERE IS THE HIGHEST RAILWAY?

In Peru. It is the **Lima-La Oroya** line, which runs from the oceanic coast and finishes almost on the roof of the Andes Mountains at 4817 metres high. Because the train rises up from sea level so rapidly to reach such a height, there are medical personnel on board with oxygen cylinders to help any passengers who do not feel well because of the changes in air pressure and the atmosphere becoming more rarefied (thinner).

Who invented the first bus?

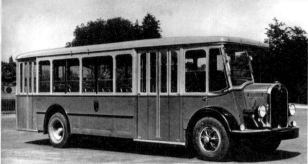

Bus built by Fiat in 1935

Julius Griffith in 1821 invented the first steam-driven bus, and this led to the first English public transport system. In 1825 **Gurney Goldsworth** patented a steam-driven bus which could transport fifteen people and had five wheels – the fifth wheel, called the **director** was at the centre of the vehicle. This model did not meet with much success, because of the poor performance of the vehicle. But in 1827, **Walter Hancock** resolved this problem and ran bus services which ran without any problems until 1839. This system of transport took passengers away from the trains and the coaches and so the railway and the stagecoach companies decided to block this competition. They waited until there was a serious accident, and then succeeded in getting laws passed which banned the driving of buses on the roads, because they said they were so dangerous.

It was only in **1897**, with the **invention** of the **first bus with an internal-combustion engine**, that this method of transport began to reach its peak.

WHO MADE THE FIRST PARACHUTE JUMP?

The first person to experiment with the parachute was the French physicist **André Jacques Garnerin**. On 22 October 1797, the brave Garnerin, after having launched his hot-air balloon into flight and reached a height of 700 metres, then let out all the hot air from the balloon and launched himself into space. When he was some metres from the ground, he opened his parachute and this enabled him to land in Monceau, Paris without breaking any bones. With the help of his brother Jean, a few years later he designed the umbrella-shaped parachute, which is very similar to that used today.

Hong Kong airport

WHERE IS THE WORLD'S LARGEST AIRPORT?

The **Chek Lap Kok** airport in Hong-Kong covers 12,480,000 square kilometres! Designed by English architect Norman Foster, it was opened in 1998 after six years of intensive work.

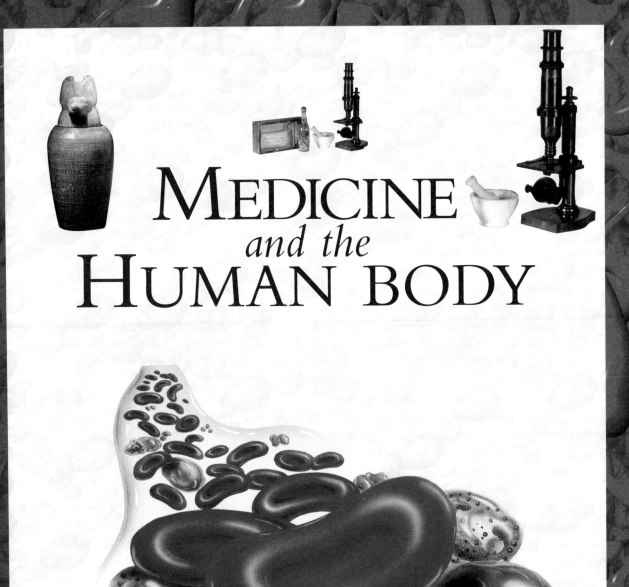

MEDICINE
and the
HUMAN BODY

When was scurvy, the 'Crew's Sickness' conquered?

In 1753, English naval surgeon **James Lind** published his *Paper on Scurvy*, in which he explained how it was that this disease made sailors so ill. **Scurvy**, Lind said, was caused by a lack of **Vitamin C** and struck mainly those sailors who had to remain for many months on board ship without the possibility of eating fresh fruit and vegetables. This led to internal bleeding, gastric and intestinal disorders and a progressive loss of weight. The first navigator to take notice of the research of Dr. Lind was the English captain **James Cook**. During his expeditions to the South Seas, he made every member of his crew, even on pain of death, eat citrus fruits and pickled cabbage, plus all other foods rich in Vitamin C – and, in fact, no member of his crew became ill with scurvy.

From the 18th century, the British Navy stated that all sailors must carry in their stores supplies of citrus fruits, such as oranges and lemons.

James Cook

SAILORS CALLED 'LIMEYS'

English sailors were nicknamed 'limeys' because they were always eating limes, a small citrus fruit grown in the West Indies and rich in Vitamin C.

Oranges and lemons are rich in Vitamin C

'SCURVY KNAVE'

As well as being the name of a disease, 'scurvy' is an adjective to describe someone who is mean and not worth knowing, the lowest of the low – hence the many references in English literature to a 'scurvy knave' meaning a low-class man.

Who was the founder of classical medicine?

Most people believe it was the Greek physician **Hippocrates** who lived between the 5th and 6th century BC. His education began in the priesthood schools where he studied texts from ancient Babylon and Egypt and built on the knowledge which then existed in countries such as Egypt and Libya. Before long he began to create a medical science of his own, based on a purely scientific approach and the facts available. Hippocrates showed that disease did not come about because of 'evil spirits' but was the result of malfunctions of some parts of the body. His revolutionary medical practice was broken down into two phases – the first phase based on **observation** of the patient and on precise **knowledge** of the person's life (such as diet, surroundings and any symptoms of illness) and the second phase structured on a **set of rules** and **a code of practice** by which to interpret the facts which had been established, leading to a sequence of **diagnostic and therapeutic tests** and then **diagnosis**. Hippocrates taught for many years at the **Medical School on the Greek island of Cos** and together with his students wrote more than fifty books on medicine, collected together in his *Corpus hippocraticum*.

Hippocrates

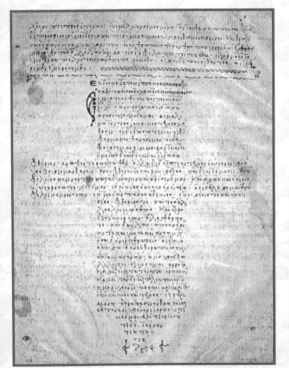

The Hippocratic Oath in a Byzantine manuscript of the 12th century

WHEN IS THE HIPPOCRATIC OATH TAKEN?

A newly qualified doctor, before beginning regular practice, has to state the **Hippocratic Oath**.

This is a professional Code of Practice which comprises a set of rules, including – to maintain professional secrets (that is, not to reveal to anyone what a patient may tell a doctor in confidence); to work with attention, skill and care for the good of the patient; to take care of sick people, without excluding anyone; and, not to carry out any acts to deliberately hasten the death of a patient.

In ancient Greece, the Oath was used as a sort of contract for those who wanted to join the Medical School of Cos.

Who discovered that germs cause diseases?

French chemist **Louis Pasteur** (1822-1895) was the first scientist to recognize that **infectious diseases** are spread through the body by **germs**. By studying and observing germs through a microscope and carrying out experiments, he proved that germs are always present, ready to strike animals and humans, especially those who are not too fussy about hygiene. He was convinced that cleanliness and **sterilization** kill germs.

Louis Pasteur

Pasteur invented the process called **pasteurisation**, which is named after him. This process preserves all liquids which are subject to fermentation, such as wine, beer and milk. In pasteurisation, milk is heated to a temperature of 100° degrees and this temperature is maintained for some minutes to kill off germs – but the process does not alter the natural qualities of the liquid, such as the taste, the smell and the colour.

Pasteur also developed a **vaccine against anthrax**, a terrible disease which infected animals and could be passed on to humans. But Pasteur's most important discovery was a vaccine against rabies, a disease which is caught by the bite from an animal. Over the years, rabies had caused the loss of many human lives, and so the vaccine was hailed by everyone as a medicine with miraculous powers.

ONE MAN'S FIGHT AGAINST SO MANY DISEASES

Louis Pasteur was a very clever man. He was appointed Professor of Physics at one University, and Professor of Chemistry at another.

Assisted by his medical team, he was able to identify and then to fight many diseases, as well as establishing an efficient system of prevention for many others, such as diptheria, tuberculosis, blood poisoning, cholera and smallpox.

Pasteur's dedication to his work was amazing. Even a stroke which he suffered at the age of 46 years of age and which left him partially paralysed did not stop him.

In 1888, the **Pasteur Institute** was founded in Paris in his honour. To this day, this Institute continues to be an **important centre for research into infectious diseases**.

The microscope and instruments of Louis Pasteur

Who discovered penicillin?

In 1928, Scottish bacteriologist **Alexander Fleming** noticed that mould had developed on one of his cultures of *Staphylococcus aureus*. Then he noticed that the bacteria which was near the mould died off, whilst the bacteria further away from the mould continued to multiply undisturbed. And so, Alexander Fleming isolated some of this mould, to which he gave the scientific name

Alexander Fleming

Penicillium notatum, and tried to develop

An orange contaminated with mould

a drug from it. But before very long, he realized that the mould substance, now called Penicillin lost its anti-bacterial strength after a few days. It was only in 1940 that, after many complex procedures, Australian pathologist **Howard Florey** and German-born British biochemist **Ernst Chain** found a way of purifying the penicillin so that it kept its effect. And so it was that the first powerful antibiotic against infectious diseases was developed, and on 12 April 1941, Penicillin was administered to a patient for the first time. In 1945, the three scientists received the Nobel Prize for medicine.

Staphylococcus bacteria seen through a microscope

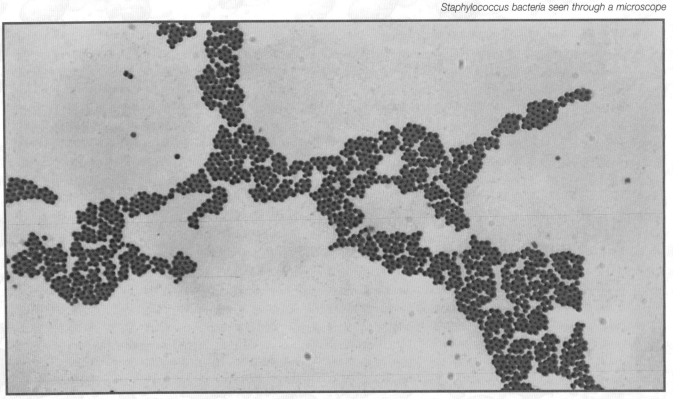

How does ear wax form?

Wax is an important **protective substance** for the human ear. It prevents dust and other small particles from getting into the inner ear. Wax is produced by skin glands in the outer ear. Ear wax is sticky, and so it can capture any 'foreign bodies' which can prevent the ear from functioning properly. Tiny, little hairs called **ciglia** prevent the wax from moving further inside from the outer ear.

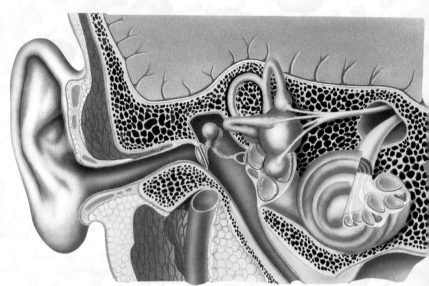

inside the human ear

Did you know...

Cotton buds can damage the ear-drum (or tympanum).

Using them frequently can alter the natural movement of the microscopic hairs (**ciglia**) and push the ear wax further inside the ear, near to the ear-drum, instead of it being in the outer ear.

WHERE IS THE ORGAN WHICH REGULATES BALANCE FOUND?

The organ responsible for the co-ordination of muscular movement and keeping balance is called the **cerebellum** which is found in the brain, in the lower rear part of the skull (or **cranium**). From one side to the other, the cerebellum measures about 10 centimetres and it weighs a little less than 150 grams.

WHY DO WE SWING OUR ARMS AS WE WALK?

As we walk, **the arms** enable the body to **balance**. Without thinking about it, we swing the right arm as we move the left leg and swing the left arm as we move the right leg. The movement of the arms keeps the centre of gravity of the body (more or less under the tummy button) at its proper position for perfect balance. As well as using the natural alternate movement of the arm with the opposite leg to maintain balance, sprinters also use their arms to push the body forward by the force of inertia (the power to move).

How is a broken bone mended?

The **broken bone** is mended by putting back in contact the fractured parts of the bone (re-alignment) and keeping the bone in this same position by means of a **splint** or **plaster cast** for at least three weeks. After one or two days, a bony material called **callus** forms and covers the fractured parts of the bone. Then cells which form new bone develop rapidly around the end of each fractured part and these new bone cells join together to mend the broken parts

There are various types of fracture. There is the **simple fracture**, when the bone breaks but the skin is left unbroken; the **compound fracture** when the broken part of the bone breaks through the skin and bone fragments can cause damage to the muscles or to blood vessels; and the **comminuted fracture** when the bone is shattered into many fragments.

WHY DO WE GO RED?

For example – when we are seen doing something we should not, or when our Prince (or Princess) Charming calls our name. But, why does it happen? Because, the part of the nervous system called the **sympathetic nervous system** prepares our body in times of stress by raising our blood pressure and increasing our heart-beat; in embarrassing situations, it sends a signal to the brain to increase blood flow to the face, and so this changes colour and we go red.

Platelets of blood seen through the microscope

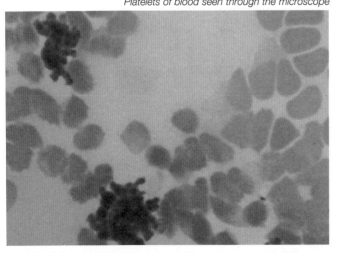

RED-COLOURED BLOOD
*Blood gets its bright red colour by a special protein called **haemoglobin** which has the task of carrying oxygen and carbon dioxide through the blood. When the haemoglobin passes through the **alveoli** (tiny air cells) of the lungs, it becomes full of oxygen and colours the blood a beautiful living red.*

Protein of plasma

97

Where do tears come from?

Tears come from **tear ducts** and **glands** (or lachrymal ducts and glands). Each tear gland is almond-shaped, and set in a sideways position just below the arch of the eyebrow. Tear-drops are mainly saline (sodium chloride). They carry out the important task of keeping the eyeball clean and moist, as well as protecting the eyelashes from dust and dirt particles.

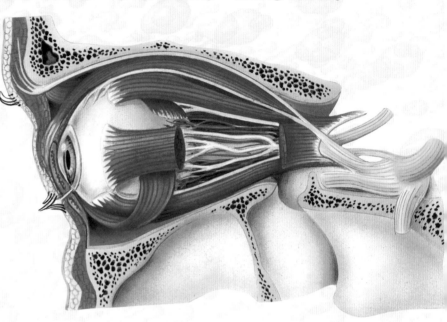

Inside the human eye

Girl with tear III, by the USA artist, Roy Lichtenstein

WHEN DO OUR EYES STOP GROWING?

The internal membrane of the eye, called the **retina**, is developing up to two years of age, whilst the other parts of the eye continue to grow until the age of six years. The eye **stops growing** completely with the **beginning of puberty** – in **males**, between **13 and 15 years old**, and in **females**, between **12 and 14 years old**.

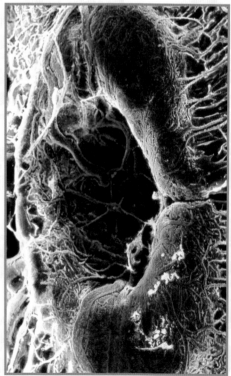

Retina seen through a microscope

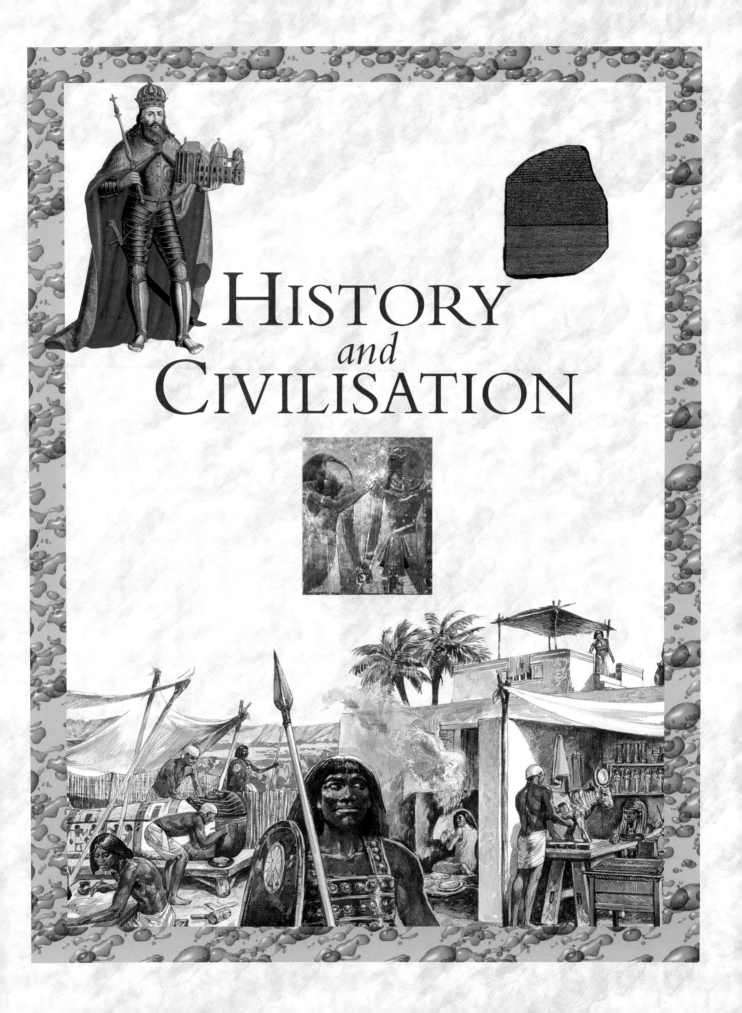

HISTORY
and
CIVILISATION

Who was Minos?

Minos was the first king and ruler of the island of Crete. He lived in the 2nd millennium BC in the famous **palace of Knossos**.

According to Greek legend, Minos was the son of the god **Zeus** and the goddess **Europa**. He was also the husband of **Pasiphae**. Minos asked **Poseidon**, the god of the sea, to make a **bull** emerge from the waters, as a sign to his enemies of his power to reign alone, without sharing his throne with his brothers. In exchange, Minos agreed that he would sacrifice the bull to Poseidon.

A bullfight depicted in a wall decoration in the palace of Knossos, Crete

Poseidon kept his promise, but King Minos forgot about the sacrifice. So Poseidon got his revenge by making Pasiphae fall in love with the bull. From their union, the **minotaur** was born, a monstrous being, half man, half bull. Minos kept the beast imprisoned in the famous labyrinth, built by the architect **Dedalus** and each year Minos had to sacrifice seven boys and seven girls of Athens to the minotaur. This cruel sacrifice continued until **Prince Theseus** of Athens entered the labyrinth and killed the minotaur.

Theseus succeeded in finding his way out of the labyrinth, thanks to the help of **Ariadne**, daughter of Minos and Pasiphae. Before he went into the labyrinth, Ariadne gave Theseus a ball of thread. Then, as he made his way through the labyrinth, Theseus unwound the thread, so that he could find his way out again.

The sacred horns, symbol of the minotaur, at Knossos

THE PALACE AT KNOSSOS

The sumptuous home of Minos was a palace with a huge number of **rooms** (more than **1000** all inter-connecting with each other), corridors and tunnels. It also had an ingenious system of carrying drinking water, consisting of earthenware pipes, one threading into the other. The windows and the large courtyards made the most of the daylight, and all the palace walls were decorated with magnificent, beautifully coloured paintings – landscapes, plants, pictures of animals, such as bulls, dolphins and the gryphon (a mythical beast with the head, breast and wings of an eagle and the body and tail of a lion), and people taking part in sports.

Inside, the building was divided into two parts, one for the queen, the other for the king. Besides all this, there were other, smaller palace residences for the courtiers, as well as shops and studios for the artists who made crockery and furnishings for the king and his court. The whole complex was more like **a small city** than a palace.

Above and to the right, two pictures of the palace of Minos
Below and left, the Megoran (private living quarters) of the queen
Right, the throne room
Below, the fight between Theseus and the minotaur in the labyrinth, from a mosaic of the 1st century BC

Did you know...

The mythical figure of the **minotaur**, half man, half bull, has interested and stimulated the imagination of many artists, writers, dramatists, sculptors and painters – to quote just a few: the Latin poet Ovid (43 BC – 18 BC) in his *Metamorphisis*, the Swiss writer Friedrich Dürrenmat (1921 – 1990) in *The Minotaur*, the Italian sculptor Antonio Canova (1757 – 1822) in his work *Theseus and the Minotaur*, the Austrian painter Gustav Klimt (1862-1918) in *Theseus and the Minotaur*, and the Spanish artist Pablo Picasso (1881-1973) in his painting *Minotaurmachie*.

When did the Mayan civilisation develop?

The **Mayan civilisation** developed around two thousand years before the birth of Christ, during the period that the historians have defined as pre-classical (1500 BC-250 AD).

They settled in a vast area which now comprises south-east Mexico, especially the territory of the **Yucatán peninsula**, **Guatemala** and **Belize**. Each Mayan city was governed by a priesthood (*halach uinic*) which included political administrators and cultural and scientific officials. In the 'social pyramid' beneath the priesthood came the **nobles** (*almehen*) who had the power of command and the privilege of private ownership within the

The pyramid of Tikai, Guatemala

territory. At the very bottom of the pyramid came the class of people which was the weakest and the least regarded – the **peasants**.

The Mayan cities were very large and could be recognized by complex architectural structures, especially religious buildings constructed in the form of pyramids.

The Mayans were skilled cotton growers and were also successful in trading, which they carried out on land and at sea. The measurement of time was of great importance to the priesthood – indeed, they drew up four types of calendar. The first was known by the name of *tzolkin* and this was based on an ancient cycle of 260 days, divided into 13 'months' of 20 days each and 18 months of 20 days, with one odd month of 5 days. The second was the 365-day solar calendar and this was used alongside the tzolkin. The third calendar, called the *Venusian* was calculated by the revolutions of the planet Venus, and the fourth, which was worked out by complicated mathematical calculations, dated from the very beginning of the Mayan civilisation. Besides all this, the Mayans worked out a system of calculation based not on units of ten, but units of twenty.

The Mayan civilisation also crossed into the early classical period (100-600 AD) and the late-classical period, 600-900 and beyond. It came to an end between 1519 and 1521, after the arrival of the Spanish conquistadores (conquerors) who reduced the Mayan civilisation to slavery.

Inca ruins at Machu Picchu, Peru

CLEVER AZTECS

The Aztecs originated from a tribe of nomads and hunters. In the 9th century AD, they settled in Aztián (hence the name aztecs) a region in north west Mexico, where in 1325, they founded their capital city **Tenochtitlán**, a name which means 'among the cactus which grows on stone'. The Aztecs were also victims of the same tragedy as the Mayans. Their flourishing civilisation was destroyed and reduced to slavery with the arrival of the Spanish between 1519 and 1521. It is said that when the Spanish, guided by their leader Hernán Cortés, reached Tenochtitlán, their king, Montezuma, innocently believed that Cortés was the reincarnation of the Aztec god Quetzalcoatl, and so Cortés was welcomed with all honours. Cortés repaid Montezuma by taking the king prisoner and seizing control of the Aztec kingdom.

The Aztec Emperor Montezuma

COMMUNICATING WITH INCA CORD

The Incas were the third great pre-Columbian civilisation which flourished in the country which we now know as Peru. As well as a form of writing, the Incas also communicated by counting, using a system called '**quipu**'. This consisted of coloured cords, each colour with a different number value. Knots were tied into the ropes or coloured discs threaded on to represent units, tens and hundreds. The system was based on a system of 7 knots and 24 different colours. The quipu was an important record, kept by government officials to take stock of goods in warehouses, as well as army officers keeping count of soldiers and judges making a record of sentences being served by prisoners.

The feathered serpent, Quetzalcoatl

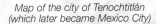

*Map of the city of Tenochtitlán
(which later became Mexico City)*

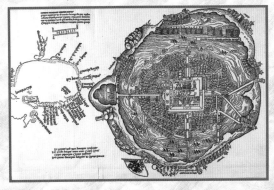

Who was Tutankhamen?

Tutankhamen was the youngest of all the **pharaohs** or kings of ancient Egypt. He was barely into his teens when he married the daughter of **Akhenaton**, one of the most powerful pharoahs, and whom Tutankhamen succeeded in 1333 BC. Tutankhamen was only 18 years old when he died in 1323 BC, but he is the best known of all the ancient rulers – simply because we have been able to learn so much about him, and the way in which he ruled and lived his life.

Tutankhamen's burial chamber remained hidden for thousands of years, until in 1922, it was discovered by the English Egyptologist **Howard Carter**. As well as the tomb, Carter brought to light a golden mask, showing what Tutankhamen looked like, his furniture, clothes and weapons. There were also texts carved in the gold which decorated the tomb, which revealed much information about the life of the ancient Egyptians.

HOW DID ANCIENT ROMAN CHILDREN PLAY?

After their lessons, boys would play with a hoop or a ball. They also played with nuts, throwing these and trying to pile them up one on top of the other to make a pyramid. Smaller children had carts to which they would harness dogs to pull them along, or they played at racing in **carts pulled by sheep**. Girls played with **dolls**, **swings** and **see-saws**. Their childhood and the time when they played with toys finished earlier than the boys – at only 12 years of age, they could be given in marriage.

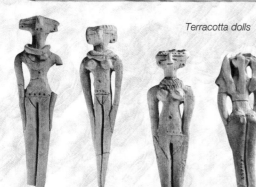

Terracotta dolls

A game of Chess

Game of Dogs and Jackals

How did the ancient Romans do their sums?

Abacus

To work out mathematical calculations, the ancient Romans used a clever instrument, the **abacus**, which is still used by young children to help them learn how to do arithmetic. The **abacus** has vertical rows of coloured balls, and each colour has a number-value – e.g. red balls for units (one), yellow balls for tens (e.g. 10, 20, 30, etc.) and green balls for hundreds. The use of paper and pen and signs for addition (+) and subtraction (–) to do sums only came into use in the 16th century, thanks to the English mathematician **Robert Recorde** and the multiplication sign (x) was suggested by **William Oughtred** in the 17th century. As for the zero sign (0) – for the ancient Romans, zero was represented by the absence of balls on the abacus.

WHO WAS THE FIRST WOMAN MATHEMATICIAN?

Teano, wife of Greek mathematician and philosopher Pythagoras (582-507 BC). She was a privileged lady for those times – women were banned from undertaking mathematical calculations – and she took over the school of Pythagoras when he died.

WHO DESIGNED THE FIRST PYRAMID?

The **first pyramid** was designed by **Imhotep**, personal physician to King Djoser in 2500 BC. As well as being Chief Minister, Imhotep was also an astronomer, an architect, a priest and a writer. He designed the **step pyramid complex at Saqquara** in Egypt. This was built as a place to house the vast tombs of the Egyptian kings. At the bottom level there were enormous rooms, courtyards, galleries and temples, with special sites for funeral ceremonies in honour of the pharaohs. The step pyramid of Saqquara was the first monument built completely of stone.

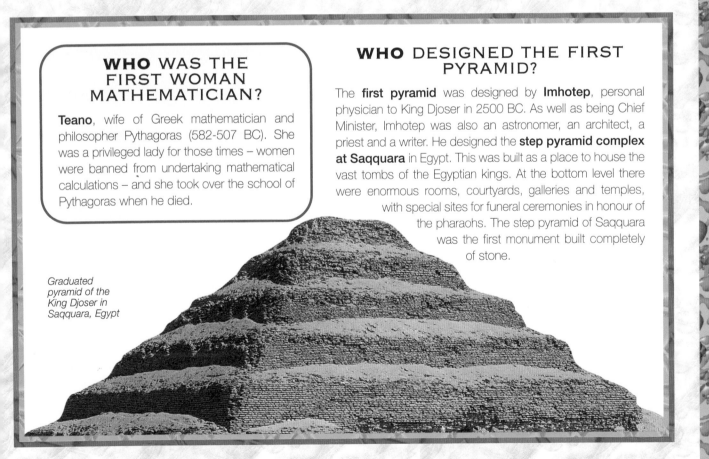

Graduated pyramid of the King Djoser in Saqquara, Egypt

When did Vesuvius bury the city of Pompeii?

The forum and the portico of Pompeii at the foot of Vesuvius

On 24 August 79 AD, Pompeii, a city colonized by the Romans from 91 BC, was completely buried by a layer of 7 metres of cinders and lapilli (fragments of volcano) produced by the **eruption of the volcano, Vesuvius**. The disaster happened just when reconstruction work was coming to an end to repair the serious damage caused in 62 AD by an earthquake. As well as Pompeii, the volcano also destroyed the twin cities of Herculaneum and Stabiae. Centuries later, Pompeii and Heculaneum became places of great interest to archaeologists. In 1748 **Carlo di Borbonne** ordered the first excavations to bring the ruins of Pompeii to light. The roads and the buildings re-emerged, revealing important information on the life of this Roman colony. In many of the noble houses recovered from the excavations and in the villas to the north of the city walls frescos were discovered which documented the Roman lifestyle from the 2nd century BC to 1 AD. The neo-classical style of European art during the mid-1700s was very much influenced by these ancient fresco pictures.

A MOUNTAINOUS THREAT

The eruption of Vesuvius in 79 AD was the first that we know about. Following this there have been more eruptions, with some of particular violence in 1631 and 1906. The most recent eruption was in 1944, and this brought about the formation of a central crater of the volcano. Cinders flew up into the air to a distance of up to 1500 kilometres, causing the destruction of parts of San Sebastiano and Massa di Somma in the provinces of Naples.

Aerial view of Vesuvius

The forum at Pompeii

A FEW SECONDS BEFORE...

The handing out of bread, as shown in a fresco at Pompeii

At Pompeii, just before the earthquake, life was going on as usual. Workers in craft studios were busy weaving wool and washing felt, cooks prepared food and drink for lunch-time, perhaps with new dishes served with **garum**, a fish sauce much appreciated by the Romans, and merchants were selling wine or a mixture of wine and liqueur in jugs. The outside walls of the houses, as in many cities today, were covered with graffiti – messages of love, insults and bits of gossip, especially about gladiators and famous people. The traffic was intense, so some stones had been placed on top of the road surface so that pedestrians could cross without stepping into mud left by horses and chariots. In fact, life at Pompeii was in full swing, until ten o'clock on 24 August 79 AD, when the eruption of Vesuvius shattered the life of the city.

When was Napoleon proclaimed emperor?

After the French Revolution of 1789, the French people needed a strong and decisive man to re-establish order. On **9th November 1799, Napoleon Bonaparte**, a Corsican-born General overthrew the government and seized power. At first, Napoleon instituted a triumvirate (three people sharing power). The three men in the **triumvirate** were made Consuls (government ministers) with Napoleon taking the role of First Consul. He reorganized the state and instituted the **Napoleonic Code**, a legal system based on Roman law. The Napoleonic Code was adopted in most countries which had been conquered by the French armies, including Italy, the Netherlands, Belgium, Spain and Portugal. Then he declared himself First Consul for life, with the right to choose his successor. Napoleon was determined to remain in power.

Even this was not enough. In **1804** Napoleon Bonaparte had himself crowned **Emperor of France**. His rule lasted until 1814, the year in which he was made to abdicate after his defeat at Leipzig and he went into **exile on the Isle of Elba** in Italy. He managed to escape, and returned in triumph to Paris on 20 March 1815. His second rule lasted only 100 days.

Painting of the retreat of Napoleon by French artist Jacques-Louis David

'The coronation of Napoleon' by Jacques-Louis David (1807)

WHERE WAS NAPOLEON EXILED TO THE SECOND TIME?

On **26 October 1915** Napoleon Bonaparte was sent into exile for the second time to the **Isle of Saint Helena**, following his humiliating defeat at the **Battle of Waterloo** (16th-18th June, 1815). The defeat against the English armies led by **The Duke of Wellington** and the Prussian armies led by **General Blücher** signalled the end of Napoleon's rule as emperor. Napoleon spent his final years as a prisoner of war at Longwood, a city on Saint Helena, and died alone on 5th May 1821.

Napoleon in exile on the Island of Saint Helena

WHERE IS THE ISLAND OF SAINT HELENA?

Saint Helena is in the southern Atlantic Ocean, near the coast of Africa. In 1502 it was discovered by the Portuguese and in 1834, it became a British colony.

The city of Longwood, where Napoleon's residence still stands, was described by the English Lord A. Ph. Rosebery as: 'a conglomeration of barracks, built to serve to shelter beasts'.

A FATAL MISTAKE AT WATERLOO

Napoleon's armies, with 120 thousand soldiers and 374 cannons, confidently went into attack against the English army of Wellington, which had only 106 thousand soldiers and 196 cannons. But Napoleon made a fatal mistake; he under-estimated **the Prussian army of Blücher**, a force he believed he had finally defeated at the **Battle of Ligny** some time before. When the Prussian troops arrived behind the French soldiers, Napoleon was surrounded. He had to surrender his army into the hands of the enemy.

The Battle of Waterloo

Who said 'I have a dream'?

Martin Luther King during one of his passionate addresses

On **28 August 1963** in Washington, Baptist Minister **Martin Luther King** began a speech which soon became famous. This began with the words, '**I have a dream**'. The occasion was a march for civil rights, in which more than 200,000 black Americans took part. The dream of King was to be able to live in the United States where people could live together in equality and brotherhood, without discrimination based on the colour of a person's skin. For many years in the USA, black Americans had not enjoyed equal civil rights to those of white Americans, and they had suffered serious discrimination (in some States, they were even made to give up their seats to white Americans on buses and to use separate bathing facilities and other public services). King fought against these injustices by organizing rights movements and protest marches, and he became one of the most followed and respected leaders of the 1960s. In 1964, he was awarded the **Nobel Prize for Peace**, in recognition not only of his work for civil rights, but also his opposition against military intervention by the USA in Vietnam. But his battles made him a lot of enemies among those Americans who remained in favour of segregation of black Americans. On 4th April 1968, Martin Luther King was killed in Memphis, Tennessee and James Earl Ray was arrested and charged with being King's assassin. But many people believed that Ray was innocent, right up to his own death in prison in 1996. For many observers in the USA and throughout the world, his sentence still remains shrouded in doubt.

"I have a dream"

'I have a dream that one day this nation will rise up and live out the true meaning of its creed: "We hold these truths to be self-evident: that all men are created equal." I have a dream that one day on the red hills of Georgia the sons of former slaves and the sons of former slave-owners will be able to sit down together at a table of brotherhood. I have a dream that one day even the state of Mississippi, a desert state, sweltering with the heat of injustice and oppression, will be transformed into an oasis of freedom and justice.'

Did you know...

Black Americans were **discriminated against in voting** by a test to see if they could read and write. Very often, they were not registered on any electoral roll, and so not technically eligible to vote. As well as this, many universities did not accept black students. Because of these forms of discrimination in 1960, Martin Luther King, with student leaders, founded an important organization for civil rights, the **Student Non-Violent Coordinating Committee**, or **SNICK**.

As well as being a politician, Martin Luther King was also a writer, and many of his works were published after his death, including – *Why we cannot wait* (1964) and *The strength of love*.

Protest march against racial discrimination organized by Martin Luther King in the city of Montgomery, Alabama

Martin Luther King on the occasion of the famous protest march in Washington, 1963

When was UNO founded?

UNO is an acronym for the **United Nations Organization**. It was founded at the end of the Second World War in San Francisco as an organization to promote peace and to encourage nations to work together. UNO is based in **New York** and now has 191 member states. The Organization has six different departments – the General Assembly, the Security Council, the Economic and Social Council, Council of Trusteeship, International Court of Justice and the Secretariat.

The five countries who had been the victors in the Second World War – Britain, USA, Russia, France and China – are permanent members of the Security Council, and each has the **right to vote** on all issues. To these countries are added a further ten, who are elected by member states and remain in power for two years. These countries may also represent nations who are not present.

The United Nations building in New York

The Secretary of the United Nations Organization, **Kofi Annan** was elected in 1997. From 1998, UNO has instituted a tribune to judge criminal charges against humanity – the **Court of the International Palace of Justice**, and this is based in The Hague in the Netherlands.

Various independent agencies operate in conjunction with UNO – for instance, UNICEF (United Nations International Children's Emergency Fund), founded by UNO in 1946. UNICEF is based in New York, and provides help to improve the health and well-being of children, taking part in programmes of long-term development in the health sector, such as health education and giving help to mothers, and there is also a programme put into operation in emergencies, to defend children against the consequences of war and other terrible calamities. In 1965, UNICEF was honoured with the Nobel Prize for peace.

The aims of WHO (World Health Organization) based in Geneva, Switzerland is to promote international collaboration in the field of research into medicines, vaccines and the battle against illness and disease.

Flags of the Member States of UNO

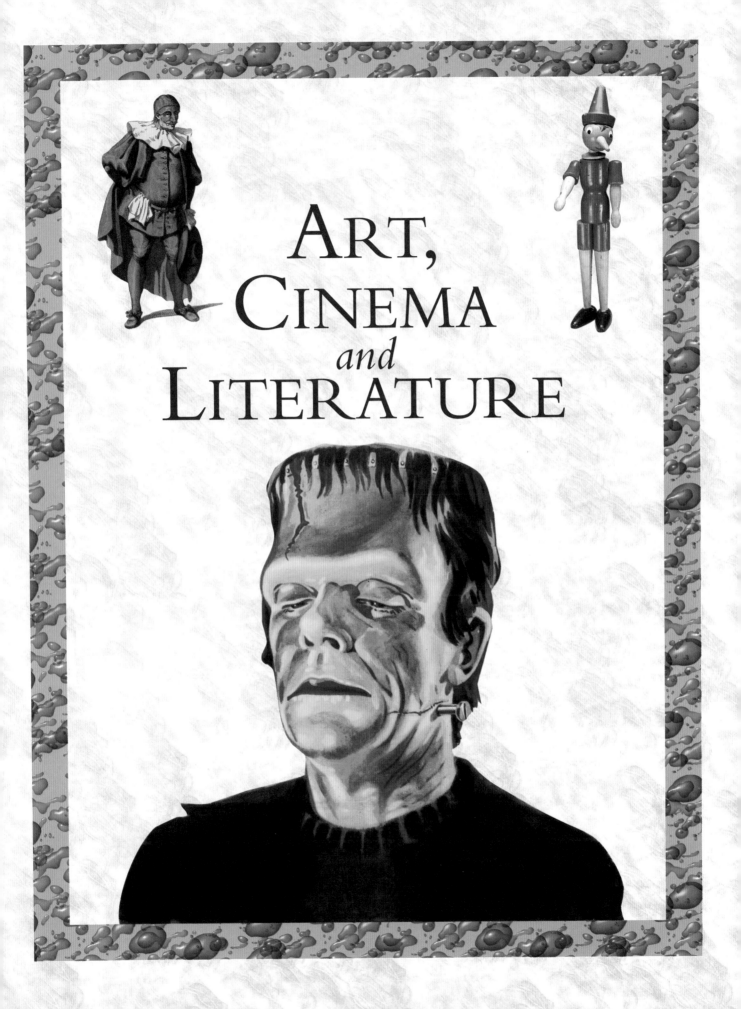

ART,
CINEMA
and
LITERATURE

When was the first Oscar awarded?

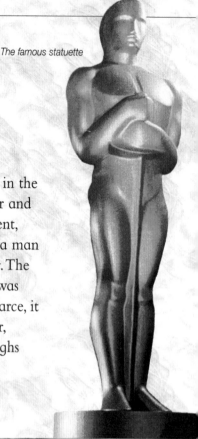

The famous statuette

In 1927, the **Academy of Motion Picture Arts and Sciences** was founded in the USA, and it was decided to give an award each year for the best film, director and actor. The President of the Academy, **Cecil Gibbons** wanted something different, rather than an ordinary winner's cup. So he suggested awarding a statuette of a man standing on a reel of film and a sword in his hands – now known as the Oscar. The first of these statuettes was made in 1928 by the sculptor **George Stanley**. It was originally in bronze, but during the Second World War, when metal became scarce, it was made of plaster. Today, the statuettes are made of a special alloy of copper, pewter, nickel and silver, and plated in 24 carat gold. Each Oscar statuette weighs 3.8 kilograms and is 34 centimetres high. 25 statuettes are awarded in many categories during the famous 'night of the Oscars'.

WHY IS IT CALLED 'THE OSCAR'?

The proper name for the Oscar is an **Academy Award**. There are quite a few explanations and theories as to how the name 'Oscar' came about - but according to the most popular theory, the statuette was 're-named' in 1931. At the first prizegiving, the secretary to the Academy, Margaret Herrick, looked at the statuette and exclaimed, 'That's just like my Uncle Oscar!'

THE FIRST OSCAR-WINNING FILM

The first film to win an Oscar award was Wings (poster shown left), a spectacular melodrama much enjoyed by pilots of the First World War and starring a very young **Gary Cooper**.

MAKERS OF THE OSCAR

At the factory of R. S. Owens in Chicago, it takes 12 people a total of about 20 hours to make one Oscar statuette. Between 50 and 60 Oscars are made each year.

A GOLDEN RASPBERRY

The same night on which the prestigious Oscars are awarded, another prizegiving ceremony takes place in Hollywood which is more disrespectful and perhaps more entertaining - the **Golden Raspberry** which is awarded for the **worst film of the year**.

When did Hollywood begin?

The story of Hollywood runs parallel to the development of the American film industry. In 1910, Hollywood was known as the **Frostless Belt**, a Californian suburb of Los Angeles, with no more than 4000 people living there. Hollywood began to develop as the centre of the cinema industry in **1911**. This was the year when millionaire **David Harsley** founded his film studio in Sunset Boulevard, the longest road in Los Angeles, and where all the major studios are today. By 1920, an average of 796 films a year was being planned in Hollywood.

Clapper Board

THE FINAL 'TAKE' OF A FILM

'**The Martinis**' is the name which some American film-makers give to the last 'take' of a film to signify the end of filming. So, when 'The Martinis' is called, the whole production team drink a toast to celebrate the end of the job and the success of the film.

97 'TAKES'

The famous film director **Stanley Kubrick** is well-known throughout the industry for being a perfectionist, someone who would make actors go through one scene dozens of times. During shooting of his recent film *Eyes Wide Shut*, it is reported that he made at least 97 takes of one sequence in which the actor Tom Cruise came through a door.

SUNSHINE ALL THE YEAR

The reason why founders of the cinema industry decided to be based in California is mostly because of the weather - the Californian climate is exceptionally dry and mild, which means that filming can be done throughout the year.

WHAT IS A CLAPPER BOARD?

The clapper board is an important piece of film equipment. The information written on the clapper board is put on film so that any editing, cutting and putting together of the film is done accurately, once the shooting of a scene is finished. The clapper board is a rectangular piece of wood with a top piece which moves on a hinge. At the beginning of each scene, this top piece of the clapper board is 'clapped' by a production assistant, who then puts the clapper board in front of the camera and calls out all the information written on it - the name of the film, the number of the scene and the number of the take, indicating the number of times that the same take has been repeated. Then the clapper board operator claps the top half of the clapper board to signal the exact start of the take, so that, later on, the different parts of the film can be put together by the film and sound editors, and the film images and sound synchronized so that these match perfectly.

The legendary Hollywood hill in California

HOLLYWOOD

How is an old film restored?

Work begins on the original negative, first cleaning the film and getting rid of ridges and small white dots by washing in solvent, then strengthening the film with a special polish. The joins made in the original editing, also the perforations for showing the film on a projector gets done again. Any lost frames are replaced by taking them from copies of the film which still exist.

Thanks to electronic technology, the sound of the film can be restored to a standard which is sometimes better than the original – so that, by the end of restoration, the old film is in new condition.

The actor Rudolph Valentino (1895 - 1926) operating a cine camera

WHAT IS FILM MADE OF?

Film is made of **nitrate**, a highly inflammable material which deteriorates rapidly, and the reason why so many films have been lost or need restoring. From the end of the 1940s to the 1990s a non-inflammable material, **triacetate**, has been used. Today **polyester** guarantees the best resistance to deterioration.

A laboratory technician restores a cinema film and undertakes the cleaning and the restoration of an old film.

WHAT IS THE ORIGINAL NEGATIVE?

This is the impression of the film at the moment it is taken, and chosen by the director to be shown as part of the film.

Containers of film are called 'reels' because of the way these are made.

When was the first photograph taken?

The first photograph in history was taken in the summer of **1826** at La Gras, France by Nicéphore Niepce (1765-1833). He photographed the courtyard of his house, seen from the window of his workroom. Today, this photograph is kept in the University of Texas at Austin. Niepce took the photograph first by sprinkling a sheet of pewter with lavender oil and bitumen of Judea - a kind of asphalt, rather like tar, which is sensitive to light, so that it hardens on exposure to light. The exposure time was extremely long - eight hours! - and Niepce called his photograph a heliograph ('light drawing'). The machine he used was made with **two wooden spools** and an **iris diaphragm** - where thin pieces of metal rather like flower petals open out and close together to control the amount of light entering the camera. This first camera of Niepce is now in the Denon Museum, France. Later that same year, Niepce presented his invention to the Royal Society, London. But as he had little documentation to record how this had been achieved and also refused to reveal the secret of his methods, his discovery was not officially recognized for many years.

Nicéphore Niepce

WHO WAS DAGUERRE?

Louis-Jacques Mandé Daguerre (shown left) was an artist and French inventor (1789-1851). He astounded the people of Paris during the first half of the 1800s with two inventions - first, the **diorama** (1822) which people still enjoy today. A painting or photograph is mounted on a large cloth, with solid objects placed in front and special lightning to give spectators the effect of actually being in front of a real landscape. The first dioramas were viewed through a hole, like a peep-show and the most famous were the panorama of Mont Blanc, the island of Saint Helena, and the view from the basilica of Saint Peter in Rome.

Daguerre's second famous invention, the **daguerrotype** was a method of taking photographs. Daguerre developed this in partnership with Nicéphore Niepce, although by the time the first daguerrotype was made in 1837, Niepce had died. First a plate of copper coated with silver was made light sensitive by iodine vapours, to form a top layer of iodised silver. After exposure to light inside the camera, the plate was removed and treated again, this time with mercury fumes, which made the areas hit by light black, to make a negative. Then the plate was 'fixed' with a solution of salt and water. This invention was recognized by the Academy of Science, Paris on 7 January 1839.

THE FIRST PHOTOGRAPH OF A PERSON
*The first photograph in which a human being appeared was taken in 1839. It was not possible to photograph moving objects or moving with the **daguerrotype**, but Daguerre succeeded in immortalizing a person by sheer chance. Whilst taking a shot of the Boulevard du Temple, Daguerre's machine captured **the figure of a man**. He was **intent on shining his shoes** and therefore remained practically immobile for the necessary time to impress the image on film. All we know about this man is that he was the first person in history to be photographed.*

The bellows of a daguerrotype

Who uses a giraffe?

The 'giraffe' is an extendable pole with a microphone attached at the top, which can be turned to pick up live sound on a film set. It is controlled rather like a fishing line by the microphone technician. It is his or her job to find a place to put the microphone as close as possible to the actors who are saying their lines, but without entering into the 'shot'.

Clap! The shooting of a new scene begins

The live sound technician in charge of the giraffe controls the levels of sound

SOUND TECHNICIAN

The sound technician is the only other person, apart from the director, who has the authority to call out 'cut!' on the set, when he or she hears a sound which is so intrusive that shooting has to begin again.

SOUND EFFECTS TECHNICIAN

When the right sound effects are lacking on the soundtrack, the 'missing' sounds are created in the studio by sound effects technicians. These technicians are able to create any sound, often using things which are found in the home.

SOUND RECORDING

Whilst a film is being made, 'wild' sounds, which some film crews call 'international sound effects' are recorded separately. These are general background noises and music, but without any dialogue. 'Ambient' sounds relating to the location, such as a tumbling waterfall or underground river also have to be recorded, and these will be used to link scenes in the film once shooting has finished.

WHERE DOES THE WORD 'CINEMA' COME FROM?

The word 'cinema' can mean many things - the place where films are shown, the collective name for the profession and art of film-making, or the general term for films. The word comes from 'cinematograph', the original apparatus for taking a series of photographs to make 'motion pictures'.

WHAT IS A STORYBOARD?

The **storyboard** shows the sequence of a film through a series of pictures of the most important scenes, together with snatches of dialogue. It is often described as a '**summary by pictures**'. Sequences are numbered and accompanied by a brief text with an indication of the order in which these will appear in the production of the film. The storyboard is very important in film-making because it provides the visual outline better than the screenplay and enables the crew to trace the main development of a film. The storyboard is especially valuable in the production of animated films, because it simplifies the sequences of scenes which require a lot of special effects.

WHAT DOES THE 'BEST BOY' DO?

Among the list of technicians at the end of a film, there is always a credit for the 'Best Boy'. We would normally use this term to describe the most clever, skilful or bravest boy in any situation. In the film industry, the Best Boy is the assistant to the leader of the technical crew.

WHAT IS DOUBLE SYSTEM RECORDING?

This is when the soundtrack is recorded on a unit which is operated by the **sound recordist**, quite separate to the cameras during filming. This system makes the process of **dubbing** easier, when the **original dialogue** is substituted by voices speaking in the language of the country where the film is being shown.

SOUND CINEMA

*To begin with, films were **silent**. Pictures used to be accompanied by a background music, played live in the cinema during each performance. The words of the actors would be shown to the cinema audience by captions and signs shown on the screen in between scenes. We have had **sound cinema** only since the 1920s when an optical recording track was added on to the film. The film which combined motion pictures with sound was The Jazz Singer directed by Alan Crosland in 1927 and made in the American film studios of Warner Brothers.*

One of the Storyboards for the film The Wizard of Oz

When was the first Star Wars film made?

Star Wars, the first episode of what was to become a great saga of fantasy, was the work of the young director **George Lucas** in 1977. It cost around 11 million US dollars to make. By the end of its first showing worldwide, the film had made 460 million US dollars at the Box Office. The first cycle of the trilogy comprised *Star Wars* (1977), *The Empire Strikes Back* (1980) and *The Return of the Jedi* (1983). The saga continued the following year with **Star Wars Episode I**, *The Phantom Menace*, shot by Lucas in 1999, which was a prologue to the events shown in the film of the first cycle, **Star Wars Episode II**, *The Attack of the Clones* in 2002 and **Star Wars Episode III**, *Revenge of the Sith* in May 2005.

Scene from the poster for the film The Empire Strikes Back

WHAT DOES 'JEDI' MEAN?

This word comes from two Japanese words 'Jidai Geki' which is the name given to plays in costume during the time of the samurai warriors of the 12th century. George Lucas invented the name '**Jedi**' during a stay in Japan whilst he was watching TV, one year before the shooting of **Star Wars** began.

STRANGE INVENTIONS

*The idea for the outline of the **Millennium Falcon**, Hans Solo's spaceship, happened by chance, when George Lucas saw a hamburger shaped like an olive during a lunch break. In the same way, the telescopic sight of the cannon laser team of the spaceship was inspired by the design of a paper-weight which Lucas had seen on the writing desk of the writer Arthur C. Clarke, author of **2001: A Space Odyssey**. The **laser pistol of Hans Solo**, played by Harrison Ford, was made by modifying an old German pistol of the First World War. The loud noises produced by the **imperial TIE fighter** were obtained by mixing electronically the trumpeting of an elephant with the recording of a car braking on a wet surface.*

RE-INVENTED NAMES

*The names by which **Star Wars** characters are known vary from one country to another. Darth Vader (which in Dutch means 'father') becomes **Dark Fener** in many European countries. In Italy, **Princess Leia** has been 're-named' **Leia Organa**. In many parts of the world, Hans Solo is called **Jan** and the two robots **C-3PO** and **R2-D2** are known as **D3-BO** and **C1-P8**.*

'INDUSTRIAL LIGHT AND MAGIC'

This is the name George Lucas gave to his team which he formed to take charge of special effects for Star Wars films. Now, 'Industrial Light And Magic' is employed to provide special effects for almost every major film studio by many of the world's top film-makers.

Who made the film 'Snow White and the Seven Dwarfs'?

This film was made by the director David Hand in 1937. *Snow White and the Seven Dwarfs* was the first **full-length animated cartoon** produced by the legendary **Walt Disney**.

It took four years to complete the film with 700 artists working full time. This animated cartoon comprises more than 250,000 separate drawings. An orchestra of 80 musicians was needed to play the background music. For all this hard work, the makers were rewarded with enormous success, plus an Oscar award for special effects. On 23 February 1939, Walt Disney, as well as the famous gold statuette, also received 7 miniature statues, one following the other in order of size - the seven Oscar-winning dwarfs!

A ROYAL LADY

The story goes that Walt Disney instructed the artist Charlie Thorson to draw up the perfect model for the character of Snow White. Thorson was inspired by the beauty of a girlfriend, an Icelandic beauty queen and former waitress, Kristin Solvadottir, who was well-known in Canada.

Who was Buffalo Bill?

His real name was **William Frederick Cody**. Born in 1846 in the state of Iowa in the USA in 1860, he became one of the drivers of the Pony Express, a sort of postal service which carried goods and parcels from San Giuseppe in Missouri to Sacramento in California. During the American Civil War, he was an explorer and a runner for the US cavalry. A brave and generous man, he became legendary above all for his accurate aim with a rifle, no matter what the target or how far away it was. Because of this and also the fact that he founded a famous circus, he was a **popular character** in the **Far West** and in **Europe** for many years. He died in Colorado in 1917 and at his funeral there were over 2000 people.

WHY WAS HE CALLED 'BUFFALO BILL?

In 1862 **President Abraham Lincoln** granted a contract to the Union Pacific Railroad Company to build a trans-continental railway from the Pacific to the Atlantic coasts of the USA. This would enable passengers to travel from New York to Sacramento in eight days. To feed the 1200 railway workers was a colossal task, and the Union Pacific Railroad Company had the idea of killing the enormous herds of **bison** which grazed freely on the prairies. Within **18 months, Cody killed** about **5,000 buffalo**, which is how he got the name by which he is still known today.

Colonel William Frederick Cody, known as Buffalo Bill

When was the 'Monster' Frankenstein created

The story goes that on the night of 16 June 1816 in a villa on the shores of Lake Geneva in Switzerland, the English poet, **Lord George Byron** and the then 20-year old writer **Mary Shelley** created the character Frankenstein after a long conversation regarding the experiments of the naturalist **Charles Darwin**. The novel *Frankenstein* by Mary Shelley was published in England in 1818. It tells the story of the scientist Victor Frankenstein who was so obsessed with the idea of creating human life that he created in his laboratory a monstrous body with super-human strength 'without soul and without name' made up of parts of various corpses dug up from cemeteries in the area. The monster was soon abandoned by his creator scientist, when he rebelled against his appearance and characteristics which prevented him from living as other human beings, and so took his revenge...

Did you know...

The writer Mary Shelley did not give a name to the creature. It was only later when the monster became more famous, that he was given the name of the scientist who created him.

THE TRUE FRANKENSTEIN

According to Christopher Goulding, a researcher at the University of Newcastle on Tyne, Mary Shelley would have been inspired by **the Scottish doctor James Lind** *to create the character of the scientist Victor Frankenstein. Lind (1736-1812) was one of the first British naturalists to carry out experiments on animals. In his laboratory, he applied electrical impulses to dead frogs, making them jump as if they were still alive.*

FRANKENSTEIN

Where do we get the names for notes of music from?

autographed score of the composer Pietro Mascagni

The first systems of musical notation are very ancient. In **Mesopotamia**, music was already being written down 4000 years ago. But in Europe, songs were passed on by voice only up to the 6th century AD. Then a system of written **notation** began to be used. This originated from **Greece**, each note becoming known by letters of the alphabet – this system of notation is still being used in many parts of the world. The notes of music used most widely today were developed in the 12th century and corresponded to the **first syllable** of the first **six verses of the hymn to Saint John the Baptist**. 'UT queant laxis / REsonare fibris / MIra gestorum / FAmuli tuorum / SOLve polluti / LAbii reatum, Sancte Iohannes' ('so that you can sing with free voice the wonders of your works, and absolve the sin, oh Saint John by your worthy lips'). It was Italian **Guido d'Arezzo**, a famous music theorist in the 11th century who noticed that the first syllable of each verse fell on a different note of the scale, and so he used the first two or three letters to name each note. It was not until the 16th century that the seventh note got a different name: SI, from the initials of Saint John (Sancte Iohannes), and in the 17th century, when the note UT was changed to DO.

MUSIC AND THE ABC

In the English or American music scores there are no words such as 'sol' or 're' marked on written manuscripts to define notes. In Anglo-Saxon countries, letters of the alphabet are used to give the names to notes - e.g. A = LA; B = SI; C = DO; D = RE; E = MI; F = FA; G = SOL.

Who composed 'Ode to Joy'?

'Ode to Joy' was composed by the German composer Ludwig van Beethoven (born Bonn 1770, died Vienna 1827), between 1822-1824. It was first performed on 7 May 1824 at the Vienna Court Opera.

'Ode to Joy' is the fourth (last) movement of Beethoven's 9th symphony in D minor, opus 125. The words were written by the distinguished German poet **Friedrich von Schiller**. He was inspired by the theme of an expression of intense joy, as a result of which people can rise above and break free of the feelings of hatred, wickedness and selfishness.

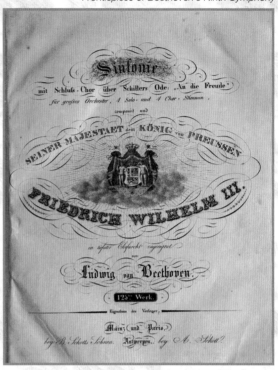

Frontispiece of Beethoven's Ninth Symphony

BEETHOVEN'S DEAFNESS

'Ode to Joy' was composed by Beethoven when he was already completely deaf. He lost his hearing when he was only 32 years of age.

EUROPEAN HYMN

Ode to Joy was adapted by the **European Union** in 1986 to symbolise the bringing together of a united Europe. Schiller's words exhort friendly brotherhood between people and between nations, a theme which is carried through in the rhythm and the melody of Beethoven's music.

Ludwig van Beethoven

Silhouette of the composer Beethoven, by the artist Schlipmann. This particular way of doing portraits was very fashionable in France during the second half of the 1700s.

Did you know...

The name Beethoven means 'yard of the beetroots' - made up of the words 'beet' which means 'beetroot' and 'hoven' which means 'yard'.

When did fairy tales begin?

All fairy tales tell stories in places and in situations without time or in an actual place. Fantasy characters are important in fairy tales. They have to overcome insurmountable obstacles, conquer over evil enemies and undertake impossible tasks, usually with the aid of helpers who are often magic or have magic powers.

Fairy tales were being told so long ago that it is difficult to say when they actually began. We do not even know who the original authors were - perhaps they were peasants and shepherds (often the main characters in fairy tales) telling stories which were then passed on by word of mouth from generation to generation, sometimes with the storytellers changing and adding extra details. They were told by grown-ups and retold by adults, not only to children, as is often believed. Fairy tales were meant to show how people should behave in difficult situations, such as facing trials and overcoming poverty, and always finishing with a happy ending. According to some studies, many fairy tales were based on pagan rites and customs which gradually fell into disuse. But the stories have survived.

The Little Mermaid

ARE FAIRY TALES AND FABLES THE SAME THING?

Fairy tales and fables are names used to indicate the same sort of literature. But the fairy tale always has a touch of fantasy, such as fairy creatures and wise animals. Fables are most often about ordinary 'non-magical' animals and they recount episodes and incidents, rather than stories. Fables illustrate the behaviour and attitudes of animals in such incidents, in order to explain a moral at the end. The best-known authors of fables from ancient times are the Greek **Aesop** and the Roman **Phaedrus**.

ANCIENT ORIGINS OF THE 'MODERN' FABLE

Some of the most famous fairy tales which we know today have very ancient origins. The oldest version of 'Cinderella' that we know about is a Chinese story written over one thousand years ago, and which then, like its writer, was already centuries old. The story 'The Beauty and the Beast' comes partly from the ancient Greek and partly from a story written by a Latin author in the 2nd century AD, 'The Golden Ass' telling the story of Cupid and Psyche.

The Little Match Girl

WHICH ARE THE MOST POPULAR FAIRY TALES?

These were passed on by word of mouth for centuries and then written down. One of the most famous collections of popular stories is *A thousand and one Arabian Nights* in which hundreds of original stories were written down in Arabic. The first person to write down popular Italian fairy tales was the Neapolitan **Giambattista Basile** (1575-1632). In more modern times, **Italo Calvino** (1923-1985) retold the Italian Fables from all areas of Italy. Among the most famous European fairy tales were those collected by the **Brothers Grimm**, who wrote down stories such as *Tom Thumb, Hansel and Gretel* and *Rapunzel*, and those by the Danish storyteller **Hans Christian Andersen** who wrote *The Little Mermaid, The Brave Tin Soldier, The Princess and the Pea,* and *The Little Match Girl.*

A Thousand and One Arabian Nights

Did you know...

The story of **Tom Thumb**, the tiny boy abandoned by his parents in a forest – or, in some versions, sold to two woodcutters – is based on true life. In the Middle Ages, peasants who could not afford to keep their children were forced to sell them.

Who were the knights of the round table?

According to legend, when **King Arthur** of England married to Queen Guinevere, she gave him a huge round table made of wood, so large that 150 knights could be seated all around it. This shape meant that nobody could be seen as being more important than the rest. King Arthur and his knights became famous, not only because of their quests and adventures, but also because they behaved according to a code of honour based on justice and truth.

The knights of the round table were seen as the most brave champions of Christianity. Among them were many famous warriors - Sir **Bedivere**, Sir **Lancelot** and his son Sir **Galahad**, Sir **Gawain** a nephew of the king, and Sir **Tristan of Lyonnesse**. The most famous of their adventures was the **search for the Holy Grail**, the cup used at the Last Supper by Jesus and his disciples and which was filled by Joseph of Arimathea with the blood of the crucified Christ. Legend says that one evening, whilst Arthur and his knights were eating around the round table, there was a loud clap of thunder in the room followed by a ray of light seven times brighter and stronger than daylight. At the same moment, invisible hands carried a cup covered with white silk around the room and a sweet perfume spread all around. Then in front of each knight of the round table there appeared the food and the drink that he preferred, before the cup vanished. King Arthur gave thanks to God for this vision and immediately Sir Gawain proposed to leave in search of the Holy Grail. When the other knights heard his words, they rose to their feet, each saying that he would do the same.

Did you know...

Some people believe that the **Holy Grail** had always been buried in Glastonbury, Somerset (England). The legend of the Holy Grail has fascinated the people for centuries. It is still being sought, because it is believed that its powers bring eternal life and everlasting knowledge.

The search proved difficult. In the end, only Sir Galahad, the young son of Sir Lancelot, was destined to complete the undertaking. Sadly, even he did not live long enough to bring this news to King Arthur's court.

French manuscript of the 15th century, depicting pictures of King Arthur

DID KING ARTHUR REALLY EXIST?

The King of Britain presented to the people by the wizard **Merlin**, who led the knights of the Round Table, who fought against the Anglo-Saxons and was killed in battle by **Mordred,** existed only in legend. It is said that the first part of the name 'Arthur' came from the word 'art' and 'hur' meaning 'rock' which in the Celtic culture was the symbol of the earth. Celtic was once the language spoken in Scotland, Wales and Ireland.

What was the 'Commedia Dell' Arte?'

Harlequin

The **Commedia Dell'arte** began in the **Middle Ages**. It was a particular type of theatre which was based on the recitation of a subject - that is to say with the author creating a play according to the surroundings - using these surroundings as scenery or a natural back-drop, rather than reading from a script. The actors had to follow the basic plot, but once on the stage, they could improvise and change the pace of the proceedings. This required perfect timing, imagination, humour and a gift for mime, because this was often used in place of words. To get good results the players needed hours of rehearsals, which were often tiring and a strain on the body as well as the brain.

Commedia Dell'arte developed from performances at town and country fairs, where people came to see acrobats, to hear the storytellers and consult 'quack' doctors. As these doctors put up their stands and put on sale their love potions and miracle cures, the acrobats would take part in little plays and sketches, miming one or two imaginary characters, while the storytellers told and sang stories, often using mime.

Balanzone, the 'quack' doctor

WHO WERE THE MAIN CHARACTERS OF THE COMMEDIA DELL'ARTE?

The main characters of the Commedia Dell'arte were all based on the old Roman tradition of men dressing as women and women dressing as men at parties and holidays - this is one of the customs of **carnival**. Each region has its own local characters, some of which became adopted by the Commedia Dell'arte. The most famous characters are - **the servants** (often called zanni) such as **Harlequin** and **Brighella**, the merchant **Pantalone**, the Spanish soldier **Matamoros**, the **Captain Spaventa**, the young lovers **Isabella**, **Aurora Flavio** and **Lelio**, the poet 'quack' doctor **Doctor Balanzone**, and **Punch** and **Columbine**.

Harlequin and Pantalone

WHY WAS IT CALLED 'COMMEDIA DELL'ARTE?'

'Commedia Dell'arte' means 'comedy of art' - but with 'comedy' meaning play rather than something funny. As well as fine acting, productions may include special skills such as stilt-walking and juggling, off-the-cuff witty remarks and a flair for athletics and mime - whatever natural talents performers have and which they can develop. The 'Commedia Dell'arte' was originally intended for ordinary people but before long it was also being appreciated by the nobles and many theatre companies with names such as *Fedeli* (the faithful) and *Uniti* (the united) were being asked to perform in the courts of Europe, particularly in France. The most famous of these companies was the **Comédie Italienne**.

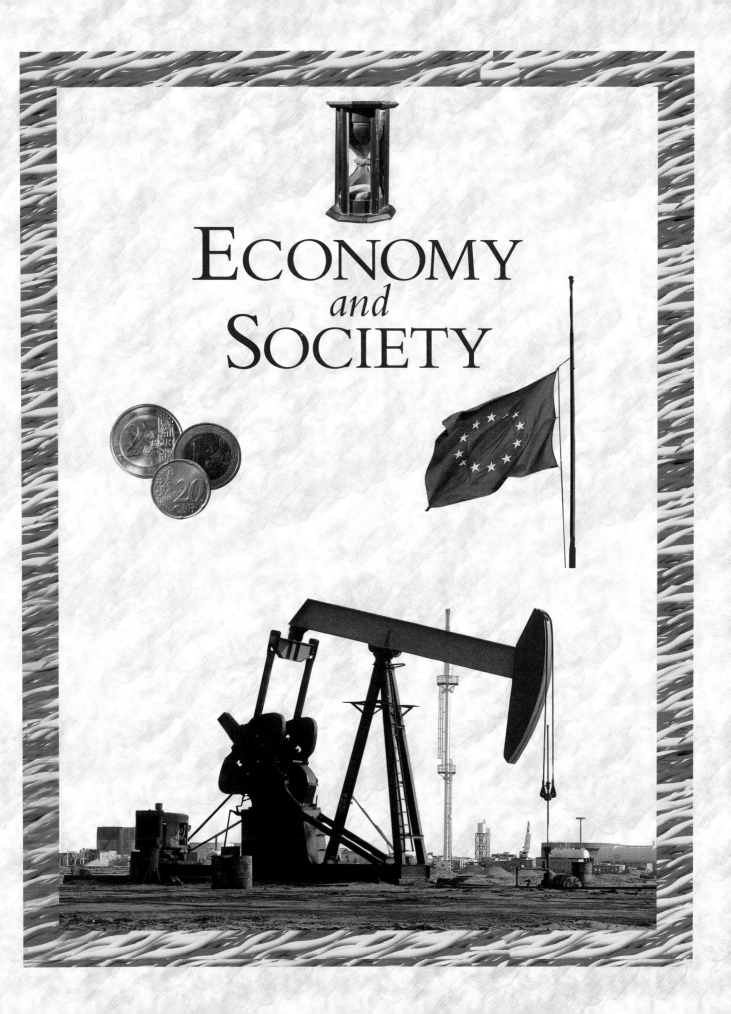

ECONOMY
and
SOCIETY

Who invented the cheque?

Before the cheque, there was the **banker's draft**. This was invented by the Knights Templar, a religious military order which was founded to protect crusaders to the Holy Land in the 13th century. The Knights Templar were often entrusted with goods and given estates by wealthy nobles from France, Spain and England and they were able to collect and transport gold to and from the Holy Land from Europe. Because of all this they soon became bankers, holding gold and valuable objects for safe-keeping, as well as making loans to nobles in difficulties and collecting the special taxes called papal tithes for the Pope to finance the **holy crusades**.

The banker's draft was used by the Knights Templar when they held goods belonging to other people. Pilgrims journeying to the Holy Land risked being robbed and so they deposited their money in the money safes of the Templars. In exchange, these pilgrims would receive a **letter of exchange**. The first 'true' banker's draft was in 1763 and was issued by **Hoare's Bank of London**.

The money-changer and his wife, painting by the Flemish artist Metsys Quentin

Geographical plan, showing the Holy Land and surrounding areas

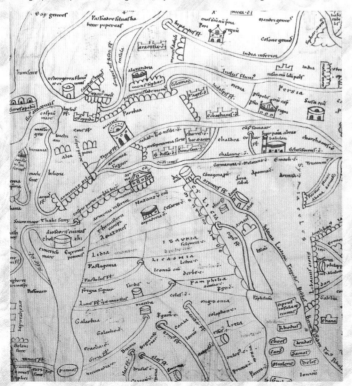

The French King Louis VII leaves for the Holy Land on the Second Crusade (1147-1149) organized by the Abbot Saint Bernard of Clairvaux

Who invented the symbol of the Euro?

The Euro symbol was designed by **Arthur Eisenmenger**. In 1975 as Head of the Graphics Department at the European Economic Community, he was given the task of making a design as a symbol to represent all Europe.

That year, he presented a sample to the European Commission in Brussels, but this remained locked away in a drawer for more than 20 years. Then in 1997, the then President of the European Commission, **Jacques Santer**, presented it to the Mint, confirming Eisenmenger's design as a symbol of the new European currency. The Euro was introduced on 1st January 1999, alongside the national currency of each country, and became the common European currency from **1st January 2002**.

WHEN WAS THE EUROPEAN UNION FOUNDED?

The European Commission was founded at the beginning of the 1950s by West Germany, France, Italy, The Netherlands, Belgium and Luxembourg. The aim was to create one single European market in order to combine the services and the strengths of these countries, thus creating a strong economy as competition against the mighty economic and powerful expansion of the Soviet Union and the USA. The European Union now has over 440 million inhabitants and is the most important commercial power in the world.

WHERE IS THE SEAT OF THE EUROPEAN PARLIAMENT?

The **European Parliament** (photograph, bottom left) is in **Strasbourg**, France. There are 626 seats. This is where proposals for new laws are presented and discussed by the European Commissioners who, together with the Cabinet of Ministers, have the power to decide which proposals should be made law. Every five years, all the people living in Europe vote to elect members of the European Parliament.

THE EUROPEAN COMMISSION

The European Commission is made up of a President and 20 Commissioners nominated by the member states. It is the ***Executive Body*** *of the European Union, and has the right to introduce new laws.*

THE EUROPEAN CABINET

The European Cabinet has the task of ***proposing new developments*** *to follow and gathers in requests from the member states. The Commission is formed of the Heads of States or Governments of single countries and the President of the Commission. The Cabinet meets every three months.*

THE MINISTERIAL CABINET

Here is where all the ministers of the member states meet together. The Ministerial Cabinet has the power to pass laws. The President changes every six months, so that each of the member states can take it in turns to handle the cabinet affairs.

Who invented the postage stamp?

The postage stamp was invented in 1840 by the Englishman **Sir Rowland Hill**, who worked for the British Treasury. In 1837, he wrote a paper which set out the details and the structure for the formation of a new postal system – the *Post Office Reform*. His project was based on three important changes; first of all, he proposed a reduction in the basic charge and said that the payment for transporting the post would be paid not by the receiver, as before, but paid in advance by the sender. Rowland Hill's idea was to set one price, an old penny, for a letter up to 75 grams in weight. On payment of the penny, the sender would receive a sticky label to stick on the letter to show that the cost of sending the letter had been paid – the first postage system. The success of the new system and its reform was such that **Queen Victoria** knighted Rowland Hill as well as appointing him Director-General of the British Post Office. Very soon, many other countries throughout the world were adopting the same postal system. In 1842, it was the city of New York; in 1843 Brazil, and the Swiss cities of Zurich and Geneva, and in 1845 the island of Mauritius and the old Italian kingdom of Regno Lombardo-veneto. The first postage stamps to be used were the Penny Black and the Twopenny Blue, both bearing the profile of Queen Victoria.

The Penny Black

Rowland Hill

MORE LETTERS WRITTEN

Correspondence increased at an incredible rate after the invention of Rowland Hill's postal system. According to statistics, in 1839 in England 76 million letters were sent. After the introduction of the 'penny post' this rose to 168 million in 1840, reaching 347 million by 1850.

Did you know...

The largest postage stamp in the world is called 'Ode to Joy – A Millennial Symphonic Poem for Mankind'. Its record-breaking size is 31 x 7 cm and it was designed to represent the world population, with the famous rock star John Lennon at the centre.

When were coins invented?

Ancient gold coins, found at Taranto

Before money came into use, trading was done by barter – exchange of goods or services. As the years passed, people began to use various objects as money – blocks of salt, glass beads, claws of wild boar and bears, animals, shells and axes of stone, and gave each object a certain value. Between 1100 and 500 BC merchandise of this type gradually changed to proper coins – round-shaped and minted from metals such as electrum, silver and gold. The first to mint silver coins with a value corresponding to the weight were the Greeks, but the use of coins soon spread throughout the Mediterranean. The word 'money' began in Rome in the 3rd century BC, because the mint, the place where the coins were stamped out, developed in the suburbs of the temple of Giunone Moneta.

King Darius and his courtiers

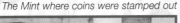

The Mint where coins were stamped out

Greek coins from the 5th century, BC

Coin stamped in electrum from the 4th century BC

Did you know...

The first metal coins were made in electrum (a natural alloy of silver and gold). These were minted in 685 BC in Lydia, an ancient region of Asia Minor. The first oval-shaped coin was minted in the 7th century BC by **King Fidone**, ruler of the Greek kingdom of Argo and Lord of the Island of Egina. This was a silver coin with a carving of a turtle on one side and which specified the value and where the coin had come from. Gold coins were introduced by the Persians. Most famous was the denarius, a coin minted by King Darius in the 5th century BC.

When did insurance begin?

Ships in the port of Genoa, from a painting of 1600

Insurance began between the 13th and the 15th centuries in the trading centres of some larger Italian cities. With the development of sea-going traffic, the merchants soon got to know how important it was to insure cargos and shipping from the dangers of the sea, the weather and shipwreck, as well as invasion by pirates. The first to issue guarantees that the value of goods would be paid to the owners if the goods were lost or damaged were the **owners of ships** who transported goods. Then the **merchants** trading in the goods became insurers themselves. The cities which first made use of this type of insurance contract were **Genoa**, **Florence** and **Pisa**. From the end of the 16th century and during the course of the 17th century, the system changed. Private insurers found that they could no longer guarantee the payment on lost or damaged goods and shipping. Instead, professional insurance companies took their place, with insurance specialists to carry out the business. Then, as the number of companies increased, they began offering insurance to protect owners of goods and property on land as well as at sea. The **Great Fire of London** in 1666 proved to property owners the wisdom of insuring buildings and valuables on land.

WHERE ARE LLOYD'S OF LONDON?

This is one of the oldest and most important English organizations in business today. It was founded in 1688 by Edward Lloyd, the owner of a coffee house where insurers gathered together to discuss and conduct their business affairs.

Did you know...

Singers **Michael Jackson** and **Bruce Springsteen** have each insured the **uvula** in their throats for around 5 million pounds. And the famous actor **Charlie Chaplin** insured his **feet** in the same way.

STRANGE TYPES OF INSURANCE

*An official of an English shipping firm insured himself at Lloyds of London for £100,000,000 for his 'mad' undertaking – **to cross the English Channel in a bath-tub!** And one religious cult has taken out insurance against being kidnapped by an alien!*

Who invented the fountain pen?

The acknowledged inventor of the fountain pen was Insurance Agent **Lewis Edson Waterman**. In 1884, Waterman was about to conclude an important contract, beating many business rivals. In honour of the occasion, he had bought a fountain pen which was already on the market, rather than a pen and ink-well. When the time came for the customer to sign his name, Waterman handed the pen to the client. But, the pen refused to write, and leaked ink on to the contract. Waterman hurried to get another document drawn up, but when he returned, he found that a business rival had secured the contract. After this bitter disappointment, Waterman invented the **fountain pen with a continual supply of ink**. This had a small hole at the base of the nib cylinder to which was attached a little rubber tube to hold a supply of ink for the pen. The filler at the side of the pen drew in a little air to ensure a steady and even flow of ink, but only when the nib is applied to the paper.

Some fountain pens have become objects of great value to collectors. The most valuable fountain pen in the world is the gold and diamond Montblanc Mesiterstück Solitaire Royal Diamond, valued at 125,000 US dollars.

Did you know...

The first **fountain pens** were filled with an ink-dropper. But with Waterman's fountain pen, the process became simplified with a **flexible rubber tube**.

Roman style ink-pots and pens from the 1st – 3rd century BC

When did banking begin?

Modern banking developed from **banks in markets** where money-changers and merchants carried out their business dealings. In the Middle Ages, the first bankers were **jewellers**. As well as keeping their own gold in safes, they also allowed other people to deposit money with them for safe-keeping. The goldsmiths issued **receipts for deposits** which soon became the first **paper money**. Each country marked this paper money with a value which was part of a proper monetary system, often controlled by a central bank. The first bank to be founded was the **Bank of England** in 1694, followed in 1800 by the **Bank of France**.

The Bankers, from a painting by the artist Metsys Quentin

WHAT DOES A BANK DO?

A bank carries out many services. As well as being a place where money is deposited, a bank makes loans to people from funds which they have. Loans must be repaid within a certain time and will be **subject to interest** – extra money, paid on top of the loan, to pay for the bank's services. Part of this interest received by the bank will be paid to customers saving money at the bank. Banks also grant mortgages for people to build or to buy property, and a Bank may also buy **government securities**. This is a way in which a government borrows money. called public sector borrowing. Funds are paid from the lender to the government, and the lender (such as a bank) will get a letter (**government security**) in exchange for the money. As well as all this, the bank may offer services to customers such as the payment of bills and the safe-keeping of valuable documents in their safe deposits.

WHAT IS CREDIT?

Credit is money loaned to a client by a bank or credit institute (e.g. a department store). The client uses the money to buy goods or pay for services, which they repay later, often by regular instalments within a certain time – 'buy today, pay tomorrow'. The bank or credit institute loaning money is the **creditor**, the person borrowing it is the **debtor**. Banks and credit institutes issue credit cards bearing their name.

The Bank of England and the Royal Exchange, from a painting dated 1851

WHO IS AN ACCOUNT HOLDER?

An account holder has an agreement with a bank, authorising that bank to carry out receipts and payments through that person's account. The **current account** is one where the customer can use cash, cheques or plastic cards to pay bills, buy goods or pay for services.

Cash dispensing machine

WHAT IS THE LARGEST BANK IN THE WORLD?

This is the **World Bank** which works with the **European Commission** and the **European Bank for Reconstruction and Development** which was founded in 1945 with seats in Washington, DC. Its members are those countries which belong to the International Monetary Fund. This Fund lends money to countries in financial difficulty, especially developing countries, to help with the creation of important projects in the interests of local people.

Bank cashier

Gold ingots

How does the 'Bank of Time' work?

The **Bank of Time** is an organization which has branches throughout the world and continues to grow. Instead of dealing in money, this Bank deals in **time**. Services and help relating to time – e.g. baby-sitting, cooking, car maintenance – are 'deposited' by account holders, to be exchanged with offers of other services or assistance. Each customer is registered with the Bank and has a 'deposit book' and a 'cheque book' to keep track of their transactions. All accounts are under the control of the Bank who see that customers do not get an 'overdraft' – taking too much time from others without giving enough of their own time in exchange – or those whose deposits are too high, e.g. piling up offers of time without exchanging time services. The agreement is voluntary, and the only obligation is to return the time which is received. The Bank of Time is regulated by the rule of **equal exchange** – offers and acceptances of time must be of equal value, taking into account social conditions (which might, for instance, result in a long or difficult journey), and economic or professional situations (e.g. a professional plumber exchanging his or her time for a wedding cake made by a student).

hour-glass

Economic negotiation in a Mauritian market

SERVICES OF THE BANK OF TIME
*The requests and offers of account holders of the Bank of Time can be among the most varied and the most fantastic, ranging from a **request for a bar of chocolate in exchange for a guitar lesson**, taking children to school in exchange for sewing to be done, small carpentry jobs in exchange for baby-sitting, watering plants in exchange for a trip in a hot-air balloon.*

AN ETHICAL BANK FOR THE WHOLE OF EUROPE

*The word 'ethical' means good conduct and behaviour. In June 2001 some banks joined together to form the Ethical Bank of Europe with the aim of promoting a system of **European ethical finance**. From this developed the FEBE 'Federation of European Banks, Ethical and Alternative' based in Brussels. Since then, many more banks have joined the FEBE, as well as banking institutes, such as the Co-Operative Bank, Nouvelle Economie Fraternelle and Caisse solidaire du Nord-Pas-de-Calais (France), Charity Bank (England), Bank für Sozialwirtschaft (Germany), Bise (Poland), Crédal and Hefboom (Belgium), Femu Qui (France and Corsica), and Cassa centrale delle Casse Rurali and BCC del Nord-Est (Italy).*

Market in Bombay, India

Helsinki, Finland

WHAT IS AN ETHICAL BANK?

The **Ethical Bank** is a credit institute which invests money deposited by their account holders solely for ethical purposes. An ethical bank will not invest in armed services, police forces, state-owned industries or oppressive regimes, where governments or businesses deny basic human rights to people. Instead, finances are focused on **disadvantaged subjects** (such as handicapped people), the conservation of the environment, and on **international co-operation for the good of developing countries**. Account holders have a say in areas of investment, and the rate of interest is stable. An ethical bank works exactly the same as any other bank and is open to everyone.

An Indian woman in the market at Jaipur, Rajasthan

Sacks of cereal, an important source of nourishment for many African populations

What are transferable securities?

The New York Stock Exchange

Transferable securities can be share certificates, deeds or bonds which have a monetary value and which exchange agents (stockbrokers) buy and sell at a stock exchange.

All transferable securities represent money lent for investment or loan on property, or a share in a business undertaking. In buying transferable securities, the purchaser takes a risk that profits on the property or in the business will increase, in which case the purchaser will share in the profits, in the form of a 'dividend' – money paid on shares, deeds or bonds. If there is no profit in the property or the business, then the purchaser of transferable securities makes a loss – sometimes losing all their investment.

The **stock exchange** is a market organization which has its own set of rules. One stock exchange will deal with others around the world. As well as deeds, bonds and share certificates, buyers and sellers also deal in gold and currency (money).

Stockbrokers at work

HOW ARE SPECULATIONS CARRIED OUT ON THE STOCK EXCHANGE?

The Latin word *specula* means 'sale' or observation. From this we get the meaning of the verb 'to speculate' – which is, to observe carefully, to make a judgement and to gain an advantage over others. In the stock market, a successful speculator – who can be an investor or a stockbrocker – will be able to see and to judge which businesses are likely to succeed in making a profit – and therefore increasing the value of shares and other investments in those businesses – and which are likely to make a loss. Very often, a loss can be only temporary, which is the chance for the speculator to buy shares at a low price with the idea of re-selling them later when their value has increased, and so making a profit.

The London Stock Exchange

The Hong Kong Stock Exchange

The Chicago Stock Exchange

WHAT IS CAPITAL?

Capital can be in the form of **goods**, **objects of value**, or **funds of money**. The owner of any capital can use it to make a profit, through their own efforts, by entrusting their capital to professionals, or by selling the goods or valuables. Where money is involved, the person lending it out of his or her capital receives in exchange an amount of interest paid by the person borrowing the money.

WHAT IS INTEREST?

Interest is the extra money paid on top of money which is loaned. It can be regarded as a 'hire charge' on money loaned and is calculated at an annual (yearly) percentage on the total capital. There are laws in place to punish anyone who loans money with interest which is proven to be too high.

The New York Stock Exchange

When and who founded OPEC?

The Organization of Petroleum Exporting Countries was founded in 1960 in **Baghdad**, Iraq by the **major oil producers**. Only 11 countries joined OPEC – Algeria, Saudi Arabia, United Arab Emirates, Indonesia, Iraq, Iran, Kuwait, Libya, Nigeria, Qatar and Venezuela. The other six large oil producers (Norway, Mexico, Angola, USA, Canada and Russia) had not given their support at that time. The aims of OPEC which is based in Vienna (Austria) are to monitor constantly the price of a barrel of oil and to promote the development of a common political economy.

The first oil well owned by Edwin Laurentine Drake

Did you know...

Almost 60% of oil was formed in ancient geological times, between 120 and 80 million years ago.

Oil refinery in Egypt

WHO DRILLED THE FIRST OIL WELL?

The first oil well was drilled in 1859 in Titusville, Pennsylvania by **Edwin Laurentine Drake**. It was about 21 metres deep. Drake, an ex ticket inspector on steamships, inserted a hollow tube into the ground in such a way that the oil, trying to keep its correct pressure, was forced to rise up inside the tube. And so on 28 August 1859 oil began gushing out of his **well**, called '**Oil Creek**' – the precious '**black gold**' signalling the beginning of the petroleum industry.

Oil Rig for the extraction of the 'black gold'

Oil well in Libya

WHERE IS OIL FOUND?

Oil is found mostly in those regions where there has been no major geological devastation – for example, in the USA, in Siberia (Russia), in the North Sea and the Middle East. In Saudi Arabia in the city of Jeddah there exists the largest service station in the world, with over **200 petrol pumps**.

HOW IS OIL FORMED?

Oil is formed by the decomposition of organic substances found in water creatures and water plants. This is caused by the action of bacteria, especially **anaerobes**, and which thrive in surroundings where there is no oxygen. From the rotting of these organic substances, there develops a mud called **sapropel**. This undergoes a process of sedimentation, where the sediment settles to the bottom, which lasts for centuries, at a temperature of 150°C and at a constant pressure until it is finally transformed into oil.

WHEN WAS OIL FIRST DISCOVERED?

The first discovery of oil was in the 3rd millennium BC in Mesopotamia, when it simply appeared out of the ground. During ancient times, oil was used as a fuel and as a sort of liniment or ointment. In the 2nd century AD, the Chinese found the first deposits of oil in the sub-soil, whilst they were drilling wells originally intended for the extraction of salt.

Did you know...

The structure for the extraction of oil was first called a **drake**. It was re-named **derrick**, because it was shaped rather like a scaffold made in 1500 in London by the **hangman Derrick**.

When did the first banknotes appear?

Below: US bank notes, value 20 and 5 dollars

Paper money was used in **China** at the time of the travels of **Marco Polo** in the 13th century. In the 10th century, metal coins were so heavy that owners had to leave them in a safe place, taking only a written statement of their value ready to exchange these statements for goods. In the 11th century, the Chinese government took control of this form of exchange and issued written receipts with a fixed value – the first bank note. Only from 1600 and 1700 did paper money spread to Europe, issued by private and public banks.

The Bank of Stockholm was the first European bank to **print bank notes** in 1661, followed by the Bank of England in 1694. But the first bank note issued and guaranteed by a government was in America. In 1690, Massachusetts issued the first **paper money** which could be used alongside coins and was **guaranteed by the State**. The use of paper money changed buying and selling – goods were exchanged for bank notes which had only a face value. Because of this, a bank note was received with a certain suspicion and caution, seen as a strange piece of paper with no value in itself, but with which it was possible to buy anything that was needed.

THE UNIVERSE
and
MAJOR
ACHIEVEMENTS

When did the Universe begin?

According to the theory held by most space scientists, the Universe began 15 billion years ago with a **cosmic explosion**, which has come to be known as the 'Big Bang'. Immediately following the 'Big Bang', the Universe began to expand and within the tiniest fraction of time, it became **1000 billion, billion, billion, billion, billion** times bigger. According to studies which have been carried out, the matter which constitutes the Universe formed at a very high temperature and very high pressure.

A prototype of the Next Generation Space Telescope

The bubble room of CERN (Conseil Européen pour la Recherche Nucléaire) in Geneva: a device which enables scientists to see the course of particles which have an electrical charge

A picture showing how we think the Universe began

THE LATEST SPACE DEVELOPMENT

The NASA (National Aeronautics and Space Administration) Space Probe **WMAP (Wilkinson Microwave Anisotropy Probe)** *can detect even the smallest variation of temperature in space (the microwave). Thanks to WMAP, NASA space scientists have suggested some corrections to important information: 1) The Universe is not* **15 billion years old** *as has been thought, but 13.7 billion years old. 2) The first stars did not first shine 1 billion years ago after the 'Big Bang' but* **only 200 million years** *after the cosmic explosion.*

ACCELERATOR PHYSICS — RE-CREATING MATTER

The main purpose of **Accelerator Physics** is to re-create conditions which were present soon after the 'Big Bang' explosion. Astro-physicists who study the Universe are convinced that at the beginning Space was composed solely of **elementary particles** and that these particles must have had their origin at the time of the 'Big Bang'. The reconstruction of the 'zero instant' at the very beginning of the Universe has been made possible by the acceleration of these particles in special laboratories. This is done by particle accelerators called **proton synchrotrons**, tubes arranged in enormous circles under the ground. Inside, the particles are made to collide with protons, electrons and other corpuscles of matter at a very high speed – 300,000 kilometres per second. As a consequence of this violent collision particles of unknown elements are formed, which would be impossible to observe naturally – in fact, these particles can only be observed during collisions of nuclear atoms at high speed.

Throughout the world there are only **five Accelerator Physics laboratories** suitably equipped for this type of study – the **CERN** (Conseil Européen Pour La Recherche Nucléaire) in Geneva, (Switzerland), the **Fermilab** (Fermi National Accelerator Laboratory), in Batavia, Chicago, USA, the **Slac** in San Francisco, USA, **LNF** (Laboratori Nazionali di Frascati) in Frascati (Italy) and the **Spring8** of Tangegashima, Japan.

When was the Brooklyn Bridge built?

The **Brooklyn Bridge** was designed in 1867 by the German architect **John Augustus Roebling** with the aim of connecting two important zones in New York – the **island of Manhattan** and the district of **Brooklyn**. Unfortunately, Roebling died before work began. And so the construction was taken over in 1883 by his son **Washington Roebling**. The length of the bridge is two kilometres and the height from the surface of the East River is 41 metres. The structure is supported by two pylons in a neo-gothic style 89 metres high, and four strong steel cables galvanized with zinc with a diameter of 28 centimetres and consisting of 5700 threads! To build the bridge, it cost 16 million dollars and the manpower was made up almost entirely of foreigners, mainly Italians, Irish and German. The Brooklyn Bridge **was opened on 24 May 1883** and many people regarded it as the eighth wonder of the world. 150,000 New Yorkers commemorated the opening by walking across what was then the longest bridge in the world.

Did you know...

It was the wife of Washington Roebling, Emily Warren Roebling who took over control of the manpower, after her husband was struck by a mysterious illness which confined him to a wheelchair. So, to all intents and purposes, Mrs. Roebling became one of those responsible for building the bridge.

Brooklyn Bridge with Manhattan in the background

When did the Eiffel Tower open?

The Eiffel Tower was opened on 31 March 1889 for the Universal Exhibition in Paris, and to commemorate the French Revolution. The design was the work of engineer **Gustave-Alexandre Eiffel**. The tower, built between the **Champs de Mars** and the **Jena Bridge** (Pont d'léna), in front of the **Trocadero** palace, is **300 metres** high and rises from a square base of 100 metres each side. It has three stages at three different heights from the ground, each one with a viewing point. The first stage measuring 50 metres each side is 100 metres from the ground and has a restaurant. The second measures 30 metres each side and is 200 metres from the ground and this is where lots of souvenir shops are to be found. The third platform is 290 metres height from the ground – and this is where visitors can see a 'tidied-up' version of the studio of Gustave Eiffel and admire the photograph given to him by the American inventor Thomas Edison. A little way above are the radio and weather stations. And from the very highest part where nobody can go, the aerials of French television rise up and these bring the height of the tower to 324 metres. The number of steps is mind-boggling – over **1792**, each one 0.16 metres deep. For the less energetic, the tower also has two see-through lifts which take visitors to the third platform.

Did you know...

The internal support and the framework of the famous **Statue of Liberty** in New York was the design of **Gustave Eiffel**.

Massive Dimensions

The dimensions of the Eiffel Tower:

Weight: 8000 tonnes

Components: 15,000 metal pieces

Cost of the work: 6 million French francs

Cleaning: every seven years for a 'new look' when the tower is cleaned of 50 tonnes of dirt.

Illuminations: 352 x 1000-watt bulbs.

Gustave Eiffel at the opening of the Eiffel Tower, 31 March 1889

What is the name of the largest star we know?

Its name is **Stella Pistol** or **Pistol Star** and it was first seen in 1997 by the **Hubble Space Telescope**.Its brightness is equal to 10 million times that of the Sun and its diameter is 300 million kilometres.Pist ol Star was formed three million years ago.It is 100 times larger than the Sun and 25 Light Years from Earth!

White dwarf star

Did you know...

The largest stars have a life which is much shorter than smaller stars. This is because they use up combustibles – energy released from heat inside the nucleus – much more quickly, due to their size.

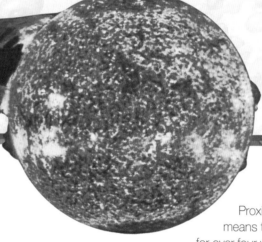

The Sun and its protuberances

WHAT IS THE NAME OF THE STAR NEAREST THE SUN?

Proxima Centauri at a distance of 'only' 4.3 Light Years from Earth. This means that, to cover the distance between us and the star, light must travel for over four years. A Light Year is the unit of measurement of the distance covered in astronomy, and indicates the distance covered in a light year – that is 9463 billion kilometres.

HOW ARE STARS CLASSIFIED?

Stars can be classified in two ways. One way is by taking into consideration the dimensions of stars, dividing them into **dwarf stars**, **average** and **super-giant**. The second way is by colour, and this classifies stars as being blue, azure, orange, yellow and red.

HOW MANY STARS ARE THERE IN THE UNIVERSE?

According to some Australian astronomers, there are **70000 million million million**!

Asteroids

METEORITES DISGUISED AS STARS
Falling stars are not stars but **meteorites** – fragments of rock which are present in outer space and which fall into the Earth's atmosphere. Here they mostly disintegrate because of friction with the air.

Did you know...

From its origins around 45 billion years ago, the **Sun** has completed 'only' 23 galactical orbits – that is, **'only' 23 complete orbits around the Milky Way!**

WHEN WILL THE SUN BURN OUT?

The Sun is still a very young star; it was formed about **5 billion** years ago and will burn out in five billion years time. This huge star is composed of **hydrogen** and **helium**. At the very centre, nuclear reactors are continuously active and these are able to produce great quantities of energy, at a temperature which reaches 14 million degrees at a pressure of 200 billion times more than that registered on the surface of the Earth. The external layer of the Sun, the **photosphere**, reaches temperatures of **5500ºC**.

Who was the first woman in space?

Russian cosmonaut **Valentina Vladimirovna Tereskova** was the first woman to journey in space. On 16 July 1963, she went up on board the spaceship **Vostok 6**, launched from the Soviet base at Bajkonur (now the city of Kazakistan). The mission was to have lasted only 24 hours, but Valentina Tereskova asked base to remain in orbit for another two days, because, at that height, she felt at ease and in perfect physical condition. In her honour, a crater on the Moon bears her name today.

WHO WAS THE FIRST MAN TO JOURNEY IN SPACE?

Yuri Gagarin (*photograph right*) Russian cosmonaut, on 12 April 1961 on board the soviet spaceship **Vostok 1** was the first man to go into orbit around the Earth, for one hour and forty-eight minutes.

Bottom left, the American astronaut Eileen Collins; below, the artificial satellite Sputnik 2

AND THE FIRST ANIMAL?

The first animal in space was the **Russian dog Laika** (real name Kudryavka) a Husky. On 3 November 1957, she was launched into orbit on board the **artificial satellite Sputnik 2**. However, because of an error in calculating the amount of oxygen necessary in the spacecraft, the poor dog died.

WHAT IS THE NAME OF THE FIRST FEMALE PILOT OF THE SPACE SHUTTLE?

The American **Eileen Collins** passed her astronaut's exam in July 1991 and **she became the first woman to pilot the Space Shuttle** on 2 February 1995. Her feat was repeated in 1999, when she flew on board the Shuttle again, but this time as Mission Commander.

WHO WAS THE FIRST TO LAND ON THE MOON?

The American astronaut **Neil Armstrong** on 21 July 1969, Commander of the **Apollo 11** Space Mission was the first person to set foot on the surface of the Moon. The mission on the Moon lasted 21 hours, 36 minutes and 21 seconds, which enabled the astronauts to collect rocks and other matter to analyse in laboratories. The second person to step out on to the Moon was Armstrong's companion **Edwin 'Buzz' Aldrin**.

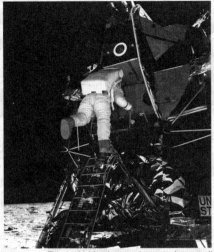
Edwin Aldrin descends on to lunar soil

Neil Armstrong

Did you know...

Neil Armstrong, Edwin Aldrin and **Michael Collins**, the Apollo 11 astronauts remained in quarantine for 21 days on returning from their mission on the Moon. This was a precaution in case they had caught any unknown illnesses.

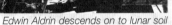
21 July 1969: man lands on the Moon

When was Sydney Opera House built?

The characteristic 'sails' of the Sydney Opera House

The **Sydney Opera House** is considered by many people to be the eighth wonder of the world. It was built over a long period of time – from March 1959 until October 1973. The building is on the peninsula which juts out from the port of Sydney, in front of the famous bridge. A great deal of intensive work was needed to build the Opera House, to say nothing of an enormous amount of money – 102 million Australian dollars, raised mostly through the Australian National Lottery. **The Danish architect Jorn Utzon** was awarded the contract to design and build the Opera House, after beating two hundred entrants from every part of the world in an international competition.

The most unusual element of Utzon's design is a dome in ten sections, each section like a sail, to form a roof rising to a height of 67 metres overlooking the port of Sydney. The domes were made of concrete, needing the support of solid arches which were not included in the original design. The construction of these arches not only raised the cost of construction by a considerable amount, they also increased the weight of the roofing. By the time work had finished, the roof was the heaviest in the world, weighing 26,800 tonnes. In 1966, Utzon, worn out by the numerous discussions and arguments about the costs, which were still continuing to rise, resigned from the project. His place was taken by a group of four architects from Sydney, headed by the **designer Peter Hall** who saw the construction through to the end. On 18 September 1973 the first performance took place, with the opera *War and Peace* by the Russian composer **Sergei Prokofiev**. The official opening, attended by Queen Elizabeth II, was on 20 October of the same year.

The Concert Hall

FACTS AND FIGURES
*The Sydney Opera House has **5 main halls** as well as restaurants, bars, rehearsal rooms, dressing rooms, a library and administrative offices. It hosts around 3,000 events each year, from symphony concerts, theatrical spectaculars, ballets, chamber music, jazz, folk and pop concerts for a total audience of 2 million visitors. The **Concert Hall** is the main venue, seating an audience of **2,679** people. It is famous worldwide for its **perfect acoustics**.*

Where is the tallest tower in the world?

The **CN Tower** in Toronto, Canada at **553** metres is the tallest tower in the world. Its height is almost twice that of the Eiffel Tower in Paris. Built in 1976 by the Canadian National Railways, the CN Tower soon became a famous landmark and a tourist attraction. Many special events take place inside, and visitors can dine in the revolving restaurant looking out across panoramic views of the city and beyond.

Niagara Falls

Did you know...

The top of the CN Tower is so high that it can only be reached outside by **helicopter**. Each year two million visitors journey to the top of the building ... in lifts!

The CN Tower

FACTS AND FIGURES

Architects: *E.R. Baldwin, John Andrews, Webb Zerafa, Menkes Ousden*

Weight: 117,910 tonnes – as heavy as 23.214 large elephants

Manpower used in construction: 1537

Number of high-speed lifts: six lifts at a speed of 22 km/h going up to the top of the tower. This offers an all-round view, and on clear days it is possible to see the Niagara Falls, 150 kilometres away.

Time taken to reach the panoramic level, at a height of 346 metres: 58 seconds.

Cost: 63 million dollars

Time taken to build: 40 months, from February 1973 to June 1976.

When will the ISS become fully operational?

The **International Space Station** or **ISS** will become fully operational somewhere around 2011 with 16 countries taking part in the project. When completed, the Station will be 73 metres long and 108.5 metres wide – the size of a football pitch. The assembly of the Space Station began in 1998 and construction has been taking place in orbit, the work being done during the course of over 20 expeditions, by American and Russian astronauts.

The ISS will be a permanent space construction manned by a team of 7-8 members, and equipped with 6 research laboratories (physics, chemistry, biology, human physiology, medicine, Earth and space sciences). It will be in **orbit at a distance of 400-500 kilometres from the Earth**. It will weigh 450 tonnes and its final cost is estimated at 100 billion dollars! The first European astronaut to reach the International Space Station in the Spring of 2001 was the Italian **Umberto Guidoni**.

BRIGHTER THAN VENUS

The ISS has a unique **module structure**, with different modules being built on to the basic bodywork by astronauts in orbit. Once completed, it will be possible to see the ISS from Earth, because of its brightness, generated by the light reflected from the Sun. This will make the ISS shine more brightly than the planet Venus.

The module structure of the ISS – International Space Station – (drawing)

How is an astronaut's suit made?

An astronaut's spacesuit has **14 layers of synthetic fibres**, made of nylon, neoprene, mylar, goretex, teflon, dacron, kevlar and nomex. These fibres are necessary to protect the body from heat (in Outer Space the temperature reaches **120°C**) and from cold (down to **minus 156°C**), from cosmic dust, from solar radiation and micro-meteorites. The **suit** has an **under-suit** which is covered by 91.5 metres of little tubes. A special liquid inside these tubes maintains a constant body temperature. To the under-suit is attached a **recycling system** for the **carbon dioxide** which is produced by the body. The space helmet has a system to supply pure oxygen and near the mouth there are two little tubes through which the astronaut can take water and food during space walks. On the shoulders is the **life-saving backpack** containing oxygen, water, batteries, communication systems, control systems and a pump for the circulation of water and oxygen. The backpack enables the astronaut to work outside the spaceship in complete freedom for several hours. On his chest is the **control junction box** which enables him to check the state of his spacesuit at any time. Also, there are four knobs which regulate the internal temperature, the volume of the radio-transmitter and the opening of the water tap.

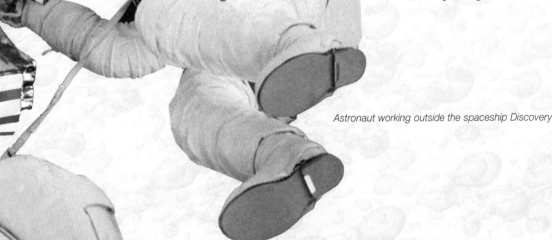

Astronaut working outside the spaceship Discovery

159

Where is the Black Stone?

The **Black Stone** is built into the eastern wall of the **K'bah**, a small shrine within the **Great Mosque** in **Mecca**, Saudi Arabia. The **K'bah** (which in Arabic means 'cube') is cube-shaped, 15 metres high, 10 metres wide and 12 metres long. It is covered in a huge black brocade cloth, the **Kiswah**. This is decorated with the Muslim profession of faith, the **shahadah**, embroidered in gold, and a new Kiswah is brought to Mecca each year. A visit to Mecca is a duty which each follower of Allah must make at least once in a lifetime. And so each year, in the twelfth month of the Islamic calendar thousands of faithful come from all over the world to pay homage and to venerate the Black Stone. There are

The centre of K'bah where the Black Stone is kept

two versions as to the origin of the Black Stone. According to one version, God sent a white stone to **Adam** when he was banished from the Garden of Eden. According to Islamic legend, **God** sent a white stone to **Abraham** when he was persecuted by evil spirits trying to drag him down into hell. To give thanks, **Abraham** built a square-shaped shrine, the K'bah, where he kept the stone – and the date of the K'Bah supports this theory. Pilgrims began coming to see it, and it became the custom for the faithful to kiss this white stone. Each time it was kissed, the stone took upon itself all the **sins** committed by the pilgrims. As a result, the white stone became black. There is a belief that the Black Stone will only become white again at the end of the world when it will return to **paradise**. A visit to the Black Stone is made according to a precise ritual; first, purification at the **sacred fountain** of **Zem-Zem**, near the K'bah, which cleanses pilgrims of their sins and cures them of anything bad. Next, pilgrims complete seven turns around K'bah before entering the shrine to worship at the stone. Each year over **one million pilgrims** gather at Mecca.

The K'bah, at the centre of Mecca

When was the last moon of Jupiter discovered?

Jupiter

In the first months of 2003, astronauts **Scott S. Sheppard, David C. Jewitt** and **Jan Kleyna** from the Institute of Astronomy at the University of Hawaii discovered **21 new moons of Jupiter**. The largest planet in the Solar System is believed to be the one with the most satellites – it has 61, whilst Saturn 'only' has 31 and Uranus 21 (satellite 22 has yet to be confirmed). The observation of satellites is done through two **powerful telescopes** installed in the observatory of **Mauna Kea** (Hawaii).

20 MOONS SO FAR

Twenty of Jupiter's satellites orbit around the planet in the opposite direction to the one in which it rotates. Only one satellite orbits in the same direction as Jupiter. They all have a diameter between two and five kilometres and it appears that they are composed of rocky-type materials, like asteroids.

One of Jupiter's satellites, Europa

Where is the City of 1000 Temples?

The city of one thousand temples is in Northern India on the banks of the sacred River **Ganges**, and its name is **Benares**, **Varanasi** in the Hindu language. The name Varanasi means 'city between two rivers' – the Varuna which flows to the north of the city, and the Assi which flows to the south – and which according to legend was the first urban settlement to be created on the Earth. For Indian people, **Benares is the holiest of cities**, and at least once in their lives they go to pray and pay homage to the gods. It is also the city where thousands of Hindus go to conclude their existence on Earth;

The god of wisdom, Ganesh

to die at Benares and to be cremated on the **ghat ManiKarnika** (in the steps of the god Shiva) the sacred place for cremation, symbolises being in the presence of God, overcoming the sorrow of death and being born again, and so having everlasting peace. Benares is bathed by the holy waters of the Ganges and here along the left banks of the river, for about 5 kilometres, are more than 100 steps, 'the ghat', down which the faithful descend to immerse themselves in the river. The city has more than **1500 temples**; the most important are – the **Bisewar**, or temple of gold, the **Durga**, and the temples dedicated to the gods **Vishnu**, **Ganesh** and **Annapurna**.

Did you know...

Cows are seen as sacred animals and so they are free to move around the city, to go into people's homes and to rest in the middle of the street (despite hindering traffic) without anyone complaining or trying to hurry them along.

The city of Benares bathed by the waters of the Ganges

What is the name of the longest wall in the world?

The Great Wall of China is the longest wall in the world. This incredible construction is about 6500 kilometres long, varying between 5 and 10 metres high, with a tower every 200 – 300 metres. Construction began in 214 BC along the northern border by the first **Chinese Emperor**, **Shih Huang-Ti** of the **Chin dynasty**, as protection against nomad tribes who threatened to invade Chinese territory. Along the top of the wall there is a road which enabled messengers to carry information and to raise the alarm at the first sign of danger. The building took ten years of intense work by 300,000 men.

CAN IT BE SEEN IN SPACE?

It is possible to see the Great Wall of China even from the Moon. However, the **taikonauta** (astronaut in the Chinese language) **Yang Liwe**, the first man to be launched into space by China, has not been able to confirm this; he returned on 15 October 2003 from his space journey on board the spacecraft **Shenzhou 5**, and said that he had not seen the Great Wall of China during his 14 orbits around the Earth.

Did you know...

The Chinese name for the Great Wall is Wanli changcheng which means 'the long wall of 10,000 li'. **Li** is a measurement of length which equals about 500 metres.

The Great Wall of China

Who named the planets?

Mosaic depicting Venus talking to Mercury

The names of the planets were chosen by the **Greek astronomers** who over the centuries carried out lots of research into the Solar System. The Greeks took inspiration from the gods and goddesses of Mount Olympus. The **planet Venus** got its name from the goddess because of its beautiful shining light. **Mars** was named after the god of war because of its red, warlike colour. **Jupiter** took the name of the most important god because it was the largest planet, whilst **Mercury** was named after the messenger of the gods because it spun so fast. The word **planet** comes from the Greek word *planetes* which means 'wandering'. The Greeks identified these heavenly bodies by noting that, in contrast to the stars which stayed in one place, planets continually changed their position as they travelled in orbit around the Sun. However, the Greeks also put the Moon into the same category – whereas we now know that the Moon is not a planet, but a satellite of Earth. The planets of our Solar System in order of distance from the Sun are: Mercury, Venus, Earth, Mars, Jupiter, Saturn, Uranus, Neptune and Pluto.

Uranus

WHAT IS THE WEATHER LIKE ON PLUTO?

It is always very cold and the winter lasts for 100 years. The temperature reaches between -228°C and -238°C. Pluto is about 6 billion kilometres from the Sun, 39 times the distance from the Earth to the Sun.

Space Probe to Pluto

WHEN WERE URANUS, NEPTUNE AND PLUTO DISCOVERED?

Uranus was discovered in 1781, Neptune in 1846 and Pluto on 18 February 1930.

Who discovered the oldest planet?

The **Hubble Space Telescope** has discovered the presence of the oldest planet in the Milky Way. This planet began about 13 billion years ago, only one billion years after the 'Big Bang', when the Universe originated. This newly-discovered planet is in the **Globular Star Cluster Mass M4**, in the constellation of Scorpius, at a distance of 5600 Light Years from the Earth. Its size is impressive – it is two and a half times larger than Jupiter (the largest planet in the Solar System) with a mass double that of all the remaining planets put together and which can contain the Earth more than 1000 times! The newly-discovered planet orbits around two stars, a white dwarf and a pulsar.

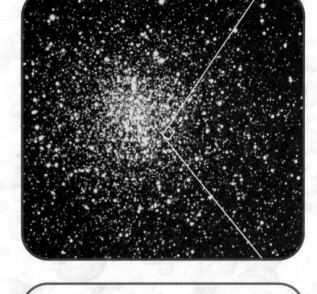

Globular Mass M4

The Milky Way

Did you know...

Compared to the oldest planet in the Universe, the Earth is still a baby! Our planet was born only 4.5 billion years ago.

Hubble Space Telescope

Where are the Voyager Space Probes?

Both the Voyager Space Probes are travelling around the **borders of the solar system!** In fact, the **Voyager 1** is 13 billion kilometres from the Sun, travelling at a speed of more than 60 thousand km/h. **Voyager 2** can be found at 10.3 billion kilometres from the Sun and travels at 56 thousand km/h. The two space probes of NASA were launched respectively on 20 August and 11 September 1977, by a **Titan rocket** and they are potentially operative until 2020. On board the two Voyager Space Probes there is a 30 centimetre copper disc on which is recorded the sounds of the Earth, animal noises, greetings in 70 different languages and 115 pictures. There is also music, such as pieces from *The Magic Flute* by Wolfgang Amadeus Mozart and *Johnny be Good* by Chuck Berry. The two Voyager Space Probes have visited Jupiter and Saturn, taking many thousands of photographs and Voyager 2 has gone near Neptune and Uranus.

Voyager 2

Voyager Space Probe near Saturn

Departure of the Space Probe, Voyager 2

SPORT

How did Basketball begin?

Basketball began in **1891** in Springfield, in the **USA**. It started with an appeal by the Department of Physical Education at Springfield University, for a fast-moving ball game to help keep the students fit during the cold winter months.

This appeal was successfully answered by a teacher, James Naismith, who came up with the idea of Basketball. The first baskets to be used were two vegetable baskets and these were fixed at a height of 3 metres and 5 centimetres at each end of the gymnasium. The first team match was played in front of a crowd of 200 people. The game was students versus teachers – and the teachers won by 5 baskets to 1.

RECORD CHAMPIONS

The most successful Basketball champion is **Michael Jordan** *who retired from the game on 23 January 1993, after a brilliant career. In 13 seasons playing for the team the* **Chicago Bulls** *he won* **6 NBA Titles.** *He also won the title of top scorer no less than ten times with an average of 31.5 points per match, the highest in the history of professional Basketball.*

When does the Davis Cup date back to?

The Davis Cup dates back to **1901**. It originated from an idea by **Dwight Davis**, a young student from Harvard University, USA. He organized a tournament between an English and an American team to take place in the fields of Logwood Cricket Club in Boston. Davis's suggestion was a challenge tennis match between teams from different countries. To commemorate the occasion, he brought 6kg of silver to a jeweller in Boston to make the now famous and prestigious **Davis Cup**, named after the founder.

The Davis Cup was first awarded to the American team, captained by Dwight Davis who became **President of the American Tennis Federation**. He later took up a career in politics as Minister of War and Governor of the Philippines.

In a little more than one hundred years, only ten countries have succeeded in winning the Davis Cup. The record for the most wins is held by the USA who have won 31 trophies.

DEVELOPMENT OF THE TENNIS RACQUET

*The **first racquets with strings** were introduced in the **15th century.** Since then, the shape of the tennis racquet changed very little. What has changed is the material with which the racquet is made. From the tennis racquet in wood with strings of catgut, we now have racquets made of synthetic materials which are light and strong – such as fibre glass, borazon (an extremely hard yet strong man-made material) and ceramic materials.*

Did you know that tennis players often have one arm longer than the other?

The forearm which holds the racquet can often undergo an **increase in the muscular mass by 30%** in comparison to the other arm. The repeated and constant movement which the tennis player makes during training and playing, causes hypertrophy – that is, the development of the muscle and the bone of the forearm.

This phenomena is apparent mostly when the player is an adolescent (between childhood and adult-hood) because at this time the parts of the body which are subject to more force than usual tend to grow more.

Where did karate begin?

Karate was first practised in the 18th century on the islands of **Ryukyu** in southern Japan. It spread to mainland Japan at the beginning of the 1900s, but it has only been a recognized sport since 1950. It is generally seen as a continuation of a traditional Japanese martial arts called **Budo**, which is still seen in some parts of the world as a way of life based on the practice of combat techniques and with the aim of physical and spiritual perfection.

The term 'karate' in Japanese means **empty-handed**. Two opponents compete in combat with bare hands, each trying to attack the other from a safe distance.

Therefore, it is very important that each opponent first hits out with fists and feet aiming for certain parts of the other person's body. Then, when one opponent comes nearer, the other competitor also uses **holds** and **throws**. The technical objective in karate is to beat the opponent in combat with one blow. Training is done by the Karate Master, the **karateka** who teaches breathing exercises to improve concentration and shows how to strengthen those parts of the body most likely to be hit by the opponent.

The Master **Funakoshi Gichin** is regarded as the father of modern karate. He defines it as a practice which enhances spiritual health.

Technical exercises based on judo

Did you know...

Judo started in Japan as an extension of the ancient martial art **Ju-Jitsu**. The founder of Judo, **Jigoro Kano**, began teaching it at the start of the 20th century, after having discounted dangerous techniques which would cause physical harm. He established the practice of wearing a white wrapper with a narrow belt in different colours according to the category that the fighter belongs to. The contenders (judoka) are classified in **twelve grades of ability**, called dan. The twelfth **dan** has been awarded only to Jigoro Kano.

Where does the word sport come from?

The word 'sport' appeared for the first time in **1829**, in a translation by the Scottish writer Sir Walter Scott from the French word *desport* meaning **entertainment** or **amusement**. The use of the word 'sport' today covers all those activities which people may play, using up energy in the process. But this expression not only encompasses the general definition of physical activities enjoyed by people since prehistoric times, but also the spirit with which these activities are carried out.

Today, even though the word 'sport' is still used to indicate competitions at amateur and professional levels, we still keep the original significance in expressions such as someone 'being a good sport' – a nice person who can take a joke.

Roman copy of the famous statue the Discus Thrower by Mirone

WHO INVENTED THE FRISBEE?

Fred Morrison, an American engineer, invented the first **Frisbee** in 1955, after having watched students from Yale University, USA throwing a **flan dish** for fun.

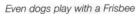

Even dogs play with a Frisbee

When did the first Olympic Games take place?

The first Olympic Games took place in **776 BC** in the Greek city of **Olympia** in honour of the god Zeus. From then on, the games were held every four years until 393 BC, the year in which the Roman Emperor **Theodosius I** abolished them.

Only men took part in the first Olympic Games, often competing in races which could be violent. In time, new disciplines were added – such as the pentathlon, discus-throwing, javelin throwing, the long jump, unarmed combat, boxing and chariot racing.

It took 15 centuries before the Olympic Games were reinstated, thanks to the French diplomat **Baron**

Ancient sculpture showing Greek competitors in unarmed combat

Pierre De Coubertin who obtained approval during an international sports congress which took place in Paris in 1894.

And so on **6 April 1896** the **first modern Olympic Games** were held at Athens, in which 285 athletes from 13 nations competed. There were twelve disciplines in the programme – fencing, gymnastics, shooting, unarmed combat, swimming, athletics, cycling, horse-riding, sailing, weight-lifting, tennis and canoeing.

Excavations of the city of Olympia, religious centre and location of the first Olympic Games.

Did you know that time was taken from dates of the Olympic Games?

The Olympic Games were being used as a point of dating reference as early as the 5th century BC. This was when a list of Olympic champions was written down for the first time by the Greek mathematician and philosopher Hippias of Elis. The system of using the Olympics as a basis for calculating time was worked out by the Greek mathematician and geographer Eratostene.

The way of working out the calculation from the date of the Olympic Games to a date conforming to our own dating system is quite simple. It is only necessary to multiply the number of the Olympic Games by 4, then subtract this total from the number 780. For example, the year corresponding to the 83rd Olympic Games is 448 BC; therefore 780 – (83 x 4) = 448. Calculation of time by the Olympic Games was used throughout ancient Greek and Roman times.

THE OLYMPIC RINGS

The Olympic flag was designed and presented to the Olympic Games Committee in 1914 by Baron De Coupertin. It has **five coloured rings** *which represent the five continents of the Earth, and the motto 'Citius, Altius, Fortius' (Faster, Higher, Stronger). The chosen colours were – blue for Europe, yellow for Asia, black for Africa, green for Oceania and red for America. The Olympic flame is lit by a torch at the start of each Olympic Games and burns continually to the very end. The torch which lights the flame is lit in Olympia then brought to the location of the Olympic Games by a relay of messengers.*

WHICH WAS THE OLYMPIC GAMES WHERE THE MOST CHEATING OCCURRED?

The least sporting Olympic Games was the third of the modern age, held in 1904 in Saint Louis in the American state of Missouri.

During the free style swimming final, the Hungarian swimmer Zoltán Halmay touched the edge only a fraction of a second ahead of the American Scott Leary – but the judge awarded the victory to Leary. This resulted in a fight between the two, and they calmed down only when it was decided to re-take the race, which was won by the Hungarian.

The Marathon was won by New Yorker Fred Lorz, but whilst he was stepping up on the podium, the judges were informed that he had been given a lift in a car for 17 kilometres.

The final of the 100 metres at the Melbourne Olympics, Australia 1956

And so the winner's medal passed to the runner-up, Thomas Hicks ; but even for him, the glory lasted only a few minutes, until the judges discovered that at 15 kilometres from the finishing line, his trainers had given him a mixture of egg-white and brandy.

The first modern Olympic Games in Athens, 1896

When did football begin?

It is difficult to say exactly where football began. In 200 BC, Chinese people played a game which they called *tsu-chu*, meaning 'to hit with the feet' *(tsu)* 'a ball of animal skin' *(chu)*.

In Japan there was a game called *kemari*, with two teams each with eight players trying to kick a ball into an area marked out between two trees.

Even the ancient Greeks played a game with a ball, called *episkyros*, which the Romans adapted to their requirements calling it *harpastrum* (from the Greek *arpazo*, to tear). It was similar to football and rugby, and was played with a ball made of paper. Then, in Italy during the Renaissance, Florentine Football began to spread. This was played by 27 men in each team.

But to find the origin of football as we know it today, we need to move on to England in 1700. Here, at the famous Rugby School, a boy picked up the ball and ran with it. After that, at Rugby, players were allowed to use both hands and feet to hit the ball – sometimes with violent contact between the players – and this resulted in **Rugby Football**. At the same time, in other places a game of *foot-ball* developed, in which the ball could only be touched by the feet – and this became **soccer** or **football**.

The **first modern football team** was founded in Cambridge, England in **1846**.

By the beginning of 1863 there were 11 English football teams, and on 26 October 1863, the first **Football Association** was established in England.

Italy v. Brazil, World Cup 1982

WHERE DID THE 'MEXICAN WAVE' COME FROM?

The 'Mexican Wave' appeared for the first time among the crowds at the 1970 World Cup in Mexico. The idea is for everyone to lift their arms in quick succession, one after the other and then lower the arms immediately. For onlookers (and those on the opposite side of the football stadium) the effect was a 'human wave' of arms, like the ripple of a wave at sea.

THE RULES AND THE NUMBERS OF THE ORIGIN OF FOOTBALL

The members of the first Football Association set down the rules of the game of football; the measurements of the pitch (maximum 120m x 90m), the measurement of the ball (0.71m circumference), the number of players in a team (11), playing-time (two halves, 45 minutes each half), fouls and punishments.
They also established that the only person allowed to touch the ball with the hands was the goalkeeper, but only if the ball came within the penalty area.

THE WORLD CUP

World Cup Football began in 1930. The first competition was organized by the Fédération Internationale de Football Associations (FIFA). Since then, World Cup Football has been held every four years, except during World War II – 1939–1945. The championship was the idea of Frenchman **Jules Rimet**, and the World Cup Trophy, awarded for the first time to Uruguay, was named after him. It was last awarded in 1970 to Brazil. This team had won the competition for a record three times in 1958, 1962 and 1970, and so it was decided that they should have the trophy permanently. The Jules Rimet Trophy was then replaced by a new trophy, the **FIFA World Cup**.

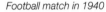

Football match in 1940

Who invented the ski?

The invention of the ski and also the sledge dates from prehistoric times. In fact, the ski is the oldest way of getting around, invented even before the wheel. A rock engraving dating from 3000 BC which was discovered on the island of Rodoy in Norway depicted men with skis on their feet. And in a peat bog in Hoting, Sweden, a pair of skis dating from 2500 BC have been found, in a perfect state of preservation.

Some explorers and historians have also identified some of the very first ski tracks between Siberia and Mongolia.
The true experts on skis were the **Lapps**. About 2000 years ago, a Lapp skier put a long, thin ski on his or her right foot, and a shorter ski on the left foot which was used as a brake and for the skier to give himself or herself a push to get started. This way of ski-ing was still being used in Lapland at the beginning of the 1900s.

Skiers in training

Did you know...

With skis it is possible to cover long distances, from 300 to 400 kilometres a day. The record is held by the Finn Rantenen with a distance of 401.28 km. The record for females is held by Sisko Kainulainen with a distance of 330 kilometres.

SKI EVENTS

Ski-ing became included in the Winter Olympic Games for the first time in 1924. At first, only men could compete in cross country ski-ing and ski jumping. Then in 1936, both men and women were allowed to take part in downhill racing and slalom (zig-zag races weaving in and out through flag-markers).
It is only since 1950 that female skiers have been able to compete in cross country ski-ing and ski jumping events.

CARVING

*'**Carving**' appeared on the ski scene in the early 1990s. It is a style of ski-ing where skiers carve out tracks in the snow. This new way of ski-ing enables the skier to bend and to curve in a very easy and effective way.*
Carving has revolutionized the ski-ing technique. Skiers use **parabolic** *or* **hourglass skis** *which are thin at the centre and wide at the head and the tail. This shape means that when the ski is under pressure of the weight of the skier, it curves almost automatically, thanks to the curved edge which grips the snow continually. This enables the skier to turn sharply and to ski at speed with improved safety.*

Descent on a snowboard

Where was tennis born?

The oldest game that we know about, which is most similar to tennis, was **jeu de paume** (game of the palm) which was played in France over 800 years ago. This was a game where the ball was patted back and forth indoors.

A Major in the British Army, **Walter Clopton Wingfield** took the basic rules of jeu de paume and invented a game which he called **Sphairistikè**, which could be played in the open air. He arranged a demonstration of the new game during a reception in the open air at Nantclwyd in Wales in **1873**, and it is from this game that outdoor tennis originated.

The American **Mary Outerbridge** introduced tennis in the United States. She had learned to play in Bermuda and on her return, she was determined to make the game more well-known. The **first important tennis tournament** was held in **1880** at the Staten Island Club, New Brighton. The matches were played on old football and baseball pitches. Until 1881 there were no precise rules as to the right equipment to use. Some racquets were triangular, others square-shaped, some curved.

The tennis balls were also different sizes. The height of the net varied, as did the size of the court. Only when the United States Lawn Tennis Association (**USLTA**) was established were precise rules and guidelines laid down.

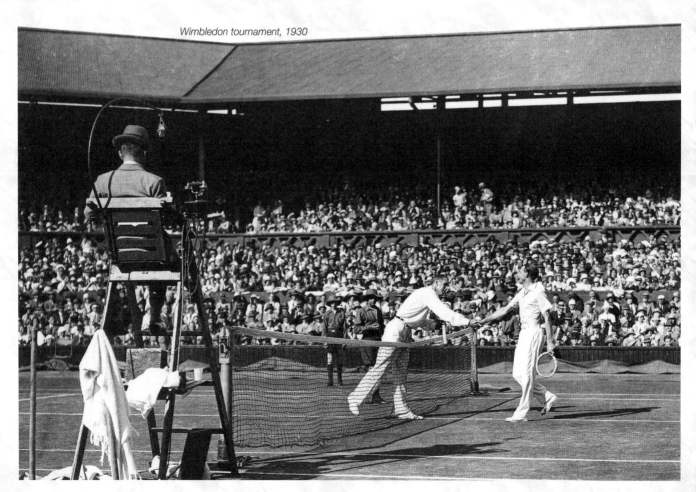

Wimbledon tournament, 1930

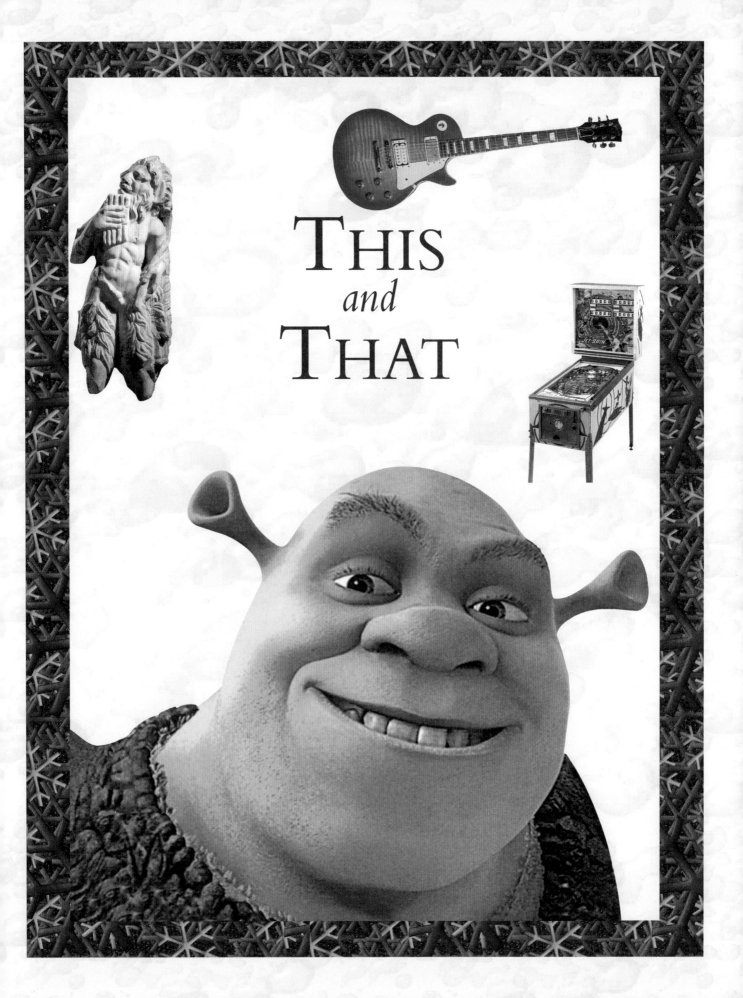

THIS
and
THAT

How is an animated cartoon made?

The first phase of making an animated cartoon is the *storyboard* – a detailed description of the story which will be brought to life on the screen. The characters, background detail, every view, each shade of light, snatches of dialogue, are all drawn on paper. The first sample of animation comes when these first drawings are mounted on rough-reels – rolls on which the storyboard drawings can be turned to give some idea of what the film will be like. If this preliminary stage of animation is all right, then each single frame is copied on to a cell – a clear sheet of acetate or nitrate paper. Once the copying was all done by hand, but today computers save a lot of time. The cells are then coloured, put into sequence and photographed, one after the other. It takes an average of 24 photographs for one second of animation. There are also photographs produced by special technology, often using the multiplane camera, developed by Ub Iwerks (Walt Disney's right-hand man). The multiplane camera uses plates of glass, each painted with different features of the animation, so that the same backgrounds, foregrounds and other features can be used throughout the production. When the 'photographic stage' is finished, then only the sound effects are missing – voices, different sorts of noises and the music. The final mounting and last-minute touches, titles – and the film is ready to show and to enjoy.

A picture of the bad-tempered ogre Shrek. This animated film was released in 2001. It was made by Steven Spielberg and Jeffrey Katzenberg in the American Dreamworks studios, which were founded in 1994. To make this groundbreaking film using computer graphics, 275 people had to work for more than 3 years.

DIGITAL ANIMATED CARTOONS

The first animator to use digital images was **John Lasseter** who created **Lux Jr.** This story of two Luxo lamps won an Oscar nomination in 1986 for the best short-length feature film. Lasseter had already been working on digital animation for some years, when he produced his first short-length feature film in 1982 for Disney. Disney was not particularly interested in this technique and so Lasseter went to work for **Pixar**, Disney's main competitor, who had been producing special digital effects for some years. Lasseter had to wait for ten years to land his first full-length digital film, the famous *Toy Story* in 1995.

WHY DO CHARACTERS IN ANIMATED CARTOONS ONLY HAVE 4 FINGERS?

Hands with four fingers are easier to draw than hands with five. This is especially true of comic cartoon characters such as Bugs Bunny, Goofy, Donald Duck, Tom and Jerry, and Sylvester and Tweetie-Pie – as well as Popeye. In full-length films which are more elaborate, human beings such as Snow-White or Cinderella, have five fingers. But the seven dwarfs have only four. It is not known which finger is missing, because, apart from the thumb, all fingers are the same length.

HOW MANY PEOPLE WORK TO MAKE AN ANIMATED CARTOON?

There are many people who take part in every single part of production. There are colourists who attend to the physical appearance and the personality of each character; photographic artists who insert any photograph which may be needed in any part of the production, and the 'clean-up artists' who have the important job of continuity – keeping track of characters, background details, and features and making sure they appear the same throughout the film, despite the fact that they may be drawn by different artists. Finally, there are the artists who produce the backdrops ('scenery'), artists who create the surroundings and technicians who supply any special effects, such as rain, lightning, thunder, shade and smoke.

Who was Pan?

Pan was the **Greek god** of forests, woods, shepherds and their sheep. According to some accounts, he was the son of Zeus and Penelope. According to others, his father was Hermes, messenger of the gods, and his mother the Nymph Driope.

Tradition says that he was born perfectly developed, with the appearance of a satyr – half man, half goat. According to legend, Pan loved wandering around the woods among mountain gorges and caves. He also loved surprising the shepherds who, seeing him and hearing his loud voice, fled with their flocks, struck by a dreadful terror. It is from this part of the legend that we get the expression 'panic attack'.

Head of Pan painted on a Roman fresco from the 2nd century BC.

The god Pan

WHAT ARE PAN PIPES?

Legend says that one day Pan fell in love with the Nymph Syringa, but she always ran away from him. One day, in desperation she ran towards the stream Ladone, praying to escape from Pan. Touched by Syringa's prayer, Ladone turned her into a rush. Not finding his love any more, Pan was near to despair when he heard the wind, whistling through the rushes and making a sad but musical sound. This made Pan pull up some of the rushes and set some of different lengths together – making the musical instrument which we now call **Pan Pipes**.

Pan Pipes

Who invented the electric guitar?

The invention of the electric guitar with a magnetic pick-up was the work of **Adolf Rickenbacker**. In 1931, Rickenbacker adapted a Hawaiin A-22 seven-chord guitar to make the basic model of an electric guitar. This was nicknamed the '**frying pan**' because of its shape. Seeing the possibilities of this invention, other performers also experimented with the electric guitar. The American guitarist, Les Paul made his solid-body guitar in 1941, removing the centre from an Epiphone electric guitar and inserting a block of maple wood on which he mounted two pick-ups. As well as this important experimentation, the name of Les Paul will always be linked with the electric guitar which he made together with **Orville Gibson** – the **Gibson Les Paul** guitar appeared in 1952 and became one of the most popular guitars of all times. Another important person in the development of the electric guitar was **Leo Fender** who designed new type of pick-up and also experimented with a solid body guitar, called the **Telecaster**. At first, the instrument was only used in country and western music, but it soon became so famous that there were long waiting lists of people wanting to buy one. In 1946, Fender founded the Fender Electric Instrument Company. Eight years later, he made his most famous model, the legendary **Fender Stratocaster** with three pick-ups and a strikingly modern design

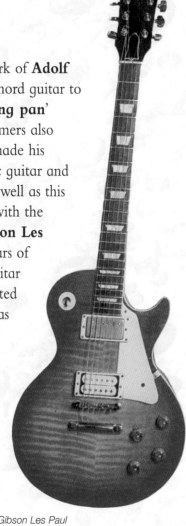

The Gibson Les Paul

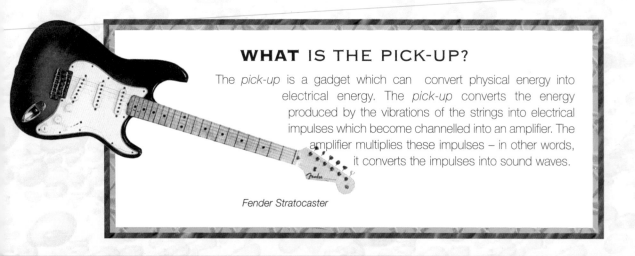

WHAT IS THE PICK-UP?

The *pick-up* is a gadget which can convert physical energy into electrical energy. The *pick-up* converts the energy produced by the vibrations of the strings into electrical impulses which become channelled into an amplifier. The amplifier multiplies these impulses – in other words, it converts the impulses into sound waves.

Fender Stratocaster

Who invented the pin-ball machine?

The pin-ball machine developed from the English game of Bagatelle. This is played on a flat piece of wood which is rounded at one end and has eight holes at various positions in the centre. At first, the player would try to get a small ball into a hole, using a little stick. Then, to make the game more interesting, the wood was tilted, and little pins were set around the holes so that the little ball could bounce off them. The development of the game continued until 1871, when Montague Redgrave mounted a spring in the Bagatelle board to propel the ball. The pin-ball machine took on the appearance which we know today during the 1930s. In the USA, enthusiasm was so great that production of the machines soon began on a large scale. In 1931 there appeared the first **money pin-ball machine** and in 1934 the **tilt mechanism** was introduced. Flippers appeared in the 1960s which players use to propel the ball towards the targets as many time as they can.

Did you know...

The first glass containers were invented by the **Egyptians** – but these were only used to serve drinks at the table and not for keeping food inside. The first glass-blown bottles appeared only in **200 BC**.

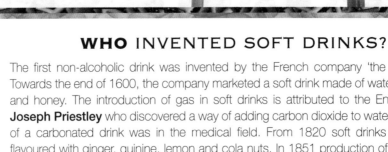

WHO INVENTED SOFT DRINKS?

The first non-alcoholic drink was invented by the French company 'the Limonadiers'. Towards the end of 1600, the company marketed a soft drink made of water, lemon juice and honey. The introduction of gas in soft drinks is attributed to the English scientist **Joseph Priestley** who discovered a way of adding carbon dioxide to water. The first use of a carbonated drink was in the medical field. From 1820 soft drinks began to be flavoured with ginger, quinine, lemon and cola nuts. In 1851 production of 'ginger beer' began, and in 1885 the first American soft drinks manufacturing company, Dr. Pepper was founded, followed by the legendary Coca-Cola in 1886 and Pepsi-Cola in 1898.

Index